AF501936

The Resurrection Narratives

THE RESURRECTION NARRATIVES

A New Approach

NORMAN PERRIN

SCM PRESS LTD

First published 1977
by SCM Press Ltd
56 Bloomsbury Street, London

© SCM Press Ltd 1977

Phototypeset by Western Printing Services Ltd
Bristol
and printed in Great Britain by
Billing & Sons Ltd
London, Guildford & Worcester

For Mircea Eliade
who first taught me that there was more to myth
than the instant need to demythologize

CONTENTS

Introduction 1

1 Approaching the Resurrection 3
- Mark, Matthew, and Luke – the differences 5
- The narratives as theology 7
- Preliminary remarks 9
- The resurrection narratives as myth 11

2 The Resurrection Narrative in the Gospel of Mark 17
- The content of the narrative 19
- The ending of the gospel 20
- The absence of appearance stories 23
- Summary 33
- The Markan resurrection narrative as myth 35
- The interpretation of the Markan resurrection narrative 38

3 The Resurrection Narratives in the Gospel of Matthew 41
- Redaction criticism as a tool in interpretation 43
- Matthew's redaction of the Markan narrative concerning the women 44
- The new elements 48
- Summary 56
- The Matthaean resurrection narratives as myth 57
- The interpretation of the Matthaean resurrection narratives 59

4 The Resurrection Narratives in the Gospel of Luke 61
- Luke's redaction of the Markan narrative 63
- The new elements 65
- Summary 75
- The Lukan resurrection narratives as myth 76
- The interpretation of the Lukan resurrection narratives 78

Conclusion 81

Postscript 87

INTRODUCTION

This book is concerned to explore the accounts of the resurrection of Jesus which have been given to us by the gospel writers Matthew, Mark, and Luke. Actually, of course, none of them gives an account of the resurrection itself; what they do is to describe the discovery of the empty tomb by the women and then, in the case of Matthew and Luke, go on to describe a series of appearances of the risen Jesus to the women and to disciples of Jesus. The Gospel of Mark has no appearance story, a matter we shall discuss in detail later. But although the gospels do not give an account of the resurrection itself, it is customary to refer to their accounts of events after the death and burial of Jesus as *resurrection narratives*. This is simply a matter of convenience and I shall follow this custom. So this book is a book about the resurrection narratives in the gospels of Matthew, Mark, and Luke.

A second point to be made before we begin our discussion is that my concern is the resurrection narratives and the gospel writers' intent in writing them. 'What are the gospel writers trying to say to us?' is the question I am constantly attempting to answer. It is my conviction that too little attention has been paid to this point, that we have tended to read the gospels as if they had been written by modern writers and not by men from a world different in some important respects from our own. But it is also my conviction that the gospel writers are nonetheless saying something very important to us in our modern world, as I shall try to show.

There are some minor points to be mentioned before I proceed. In the first place, the technical term for 'gospel writer' in use among scholars is 'evangelist', and I shall tend to use this word of Matthew, Mark, and Luke simply in the sense of 'gospel writer'. Then, further, I use the names 'Matthew', 'Mark', and 'Luke' as a matter of convenience, without intending thereby to make any statement with regard to the authorship of the gospels of Matthew and Mark, or of the two-volume work Luke–Acts. Each of these works is the product of an author with a distinctive theological viewpoint, and it is these theological viewpoints which concern us. All the works were originally written and circulated anonymously. Names were attributed to them only in later ecclesiastical tradition. How accurate that tradition was in the matter of names is a matter of the most complete indifference compared to the coherence and integrity of the theological viewpoint of the works themselves. Lastly, all quotations from the Bible are from the Revised Standard Version (Second Edition of the New Testament 1971) unless otherwise noted.

1

APPROACHING THE RESURRECTION

How does one read the resurrection narratives? With what kind of expectation of experienceable reality does one approach the story of the women at the empty tomb in the Gospel of Mark, or that of the two disciples on the Emmaus road in the Gospel of Luke? There can be few Christians who have not read these stories – or perhaps heard them read in the context of an Easter morning service – and found themselves affirming them with heart and soul and mind. We live and move and have our being in a world in which Jesus is risen from the dead. A quality of life is possible for us in that world which would not be possible for us without the faith we celebrate each Easter morning. 'Jesus is risen!' we cry, and we share his victory over the last enemy, death.

Mark, Matthew, and Luke – the differences

So the resurrection narratives in the gospels are meaningful to us as the affirmation of a possibility for our life in the world, and in the context of an Easter morning service they ring true and clear. But suppose we take them out of that particular context and put them in another and quite different one, namely, in that of a critical historian's study. What happens then? It does not even need to be a particularly critical historian. Anyone who has ever written a report or an essay for a history class in school or college can see immediately that there are glaring discrepancies among the resurrection narratives in the gospels. In the Gospel of Mark the women are addressed at the empty tomb by 'a young man dressed in a white robe'; in the gospel of Matthew this young man becomes 'an angel of the Lord from heaven' whose 'appearance was like lightning and his raiment white as snow'; in the Gospel of Luke he becomes 'two men in dazzling apparel'. In the Gospel of Mark, the women say nothing to anyone, 'for they were afraid'; in the Gospel of Luke they return from the tomb and tell 'all this to the eleven and to all the rest'.

Discrepancies like this are not terribly important in themselves. The gospels were, after all, written some forty or fifty years after the event, and stories of momentous events grow in the telling. As we shall see, some of the differences among the gospel narratives of the resurrection are best understood as the consequence of stories growing in the telling. But there are other and more important differences among the gospels in connection with the resurrection of Jesus. Above all, there are the differences with regard to the appearance of the risen Jesus to his followers. In the Gospel of Mark, which originally ended at what is now chapter 16, verse 8, the risen Jesus does *not* appear to anyone *at all*. In the Gospel of Matthew he appears to his disciples *only in Galilee*; and in the Gospel of Luke he appears *only in Jerusalem* and its environs. Alerted by this fact, and it *is* a fact, the attentive reader will go on to recognize that each of the gospel writers, the evangelists, has his own particular and distinctive understanding of the nature of the resurrection of Jesus, and that the discrepancies are a consequence of these different understandings. I hope to be able to show in the course of the following chapters that Mark understands the resurrection of Jesus as God having vindicated Jesus out of his death by taking him 'up' into heaven to be with him until the time of Jesus' return to earth as Son of man, to judge and to redeem the world. Matthew, on the other hand, thinks of Jesus as having been taken up by God into heaven, but then as appearing to his disciples in Galilee, as it were proleptically, in anticipation of his final glory, having been given 'all authority in heaven and on earth', and as founding the church by virtue of his authority. Luke, by contrast, conceives of Jesus as having appeared to his disciples in bodily form in and around Jerusalem as a man indistinguishable from other men, except insofar as one could recognize him personally, as instructing his disciples in their new responsibilities for the spread of the gospel in the world, and as then being transported bodily into the heavens.

The narratives as theology

The details of the individual evangelists' understanding of the resurrection will concern us later. What concerns us now is the fact that each does understand the resurrection differently, and that each expresses his understanding in the narrative as he writes. The resurrection narratives are, in other words, literary expressions of the evangelists' understanding of what it means to say 'Jesus is risen!' They are narrative expressions of a distinctive theological viewpoint. But then this is true of the gospels as a whole. Each narrative in a gospel is to a greater or lesser extent a literary expression of the theological viewpoint of the evangelist concerned. Each evangelist chose to retell stories about Jesus – to compose a narrative account of the life and fate of Jesus. The first of them, Mark, made his intention quite clear by beginning his account with the rubric, 'The beginning of the gospel of Jesus Christ, the Son of God' (1.1). The 'gospel' is the proclamation of the 'good news', the good news of what God has done for man through his son Jesus – and Jesus is both Christ, that is, the Messiah promised to the Jewish people, and Son of God, that is, one who stands in such a relationship to God himself that his life and fate change for ever the possibilities of man's relationship to God, and hence the possibilities for human life in the world.

It would be hard to imagine a more theologically loaded statement than the first verse of the Gospel of Mark, and in penning it the evangelist is alerting his readers to the intent of his narrative as a whole. He intends to convince his readers that Jesus is the Messiah, that he is Son of God, and that his life and fate have changed for ever the possibilities for human life in the world. To this end he composes his narrative account of the sequence of events which began with the ministry of John the Baptist, continued through the ministry of Jesus, and reached its climax in the women's discovery of the empty tomb. He has taken traditional material circulating in the early Christian communities about John the Baptist and about Jesus and his disciples; he has edited that material and composed it into a new whole – he may even have created some new narratives of his own on the basis of traditional sayings of Jesus and interpretation of scripture – and everything that he has done, he has done in the service of his over-riding conviction that he has a gospel to preach to his readers: the good news of what God has wrought for man through his Son, Jesus the long-awaited Jewish Messiah.

Nor does this attitude towards, and use of, gospel narratives end with the evangelist Mark. Both Matthew and Luke echo and imitate the practice of Mark. They each take the narratives of the Gospel of Mark, and other traditional material to which each has access, and they edit this material; they compose it into a new whole – probably also creating new narratives of their own on the basis of traditional sayings of Jesus and interpretations of scripture – and they do this in the service of their own particular understanding of what it is that God has done through his Son, Jesus the long-awaited Jewish Messiah, that has changed for ever the possibilities for human life in the world. True, they do not use the word *gospel* in their superscriptions as does Mark; Matthew 1.1 uses the word *book*, and Luke 1.1, *narrative*. But even this change is theologically motivated. As we shall see, Matthew is enormously concerned with the idea of verbal revelation, and hence turns naturally to the word *book*, whereas Luke's overwhelming concern is the fate-laden journey of Jesus to his death and resurrection in Jerusalem, and the spread of the Christian gospel from Jerusalem to Rome. Hence, for him, *narrative* is an appropriate term. But whether called gospel, book, or narrative, the works written by the evangelists Mark, Matthew, and Luke are above all literary expressions of the theological convictions of their authors, and the often divergent details of their stories become important to us as indices of these theological convictions, as indications of deeply held beliefs regarding the status of man in the world and before God as a consequence of the life and fate of Jesus of Nazareth.

The consequence of this view of the gospel narratives is both immediate and far reaching. Now we no longer ask ourselves, 'Did Jesus appear as risen from the dead to his disciples not at all (so Mark), or in Galilee (so Matthew), or only in Jerusalem and its environs (so Luke)?' Instead we ask ourselves, 'What is Mark trying to say to us by deliberately omitting appearance stories, or Matthew by locating the major appearance in Galilee, or Luke by limiting appearances to the Jerusalem area?' These are the questions that matter because they are questions about the motivations and convictions of the evangelists themselves; they are questions about the challenges which the writers of the gospels deliberately put to their readers – including ourselves. For far too long we modern readers of the gospels have allowed our attention to be diverted from the true intention of the gospel narratives by constantly asking the historical question, 'What actually happened?', instead of asking the evangelical question, 'What is it that the gospel writer is challenging us to accept or to deny by means of this particular narrative?' The chapters that follow are a deliberate attempt to redress this balance. They approach the resurrection narratives from the standpoint of the questions, 'What is the evangelist trying to say to us by writing as he does?' 'What is he challenging us to accept or to deny?'

Preliminary remarks

Before proceeding to a discussion of the resurrection narratives themselves, some further preliminary remarks are in order.

In what follows I shall discuss the resurrection narratives

in the Gospels of Mark, Matthew, and Luke, that is, in the synoptic gospels. I shall not discuss the resurrection narratives in the Gospel of John for the good and sufficient reason that I lack the scholarly competence to do so. In these days of increasing scholarly knowledge and specialization the differences between research in the synoptic gospels and the Gospel of John are such that I, having spent my academic life in synoptic gospel research, simply could not write about the Gospel of John with the degree of sureness that would be required of me. So the following discussion, because of the limitations of my own scholarly competence, deals only with the resurrection narratives in the synoptic gospels.

The following discussion also does not include any extended treatment of the narrative in the Acts of the Apostles (1.3–11). The reason for this is that it is not formally, that is, so far as its form is concerned, a resurrection narrative. The gospel of Luke–Acts of the Apostles is, of course, one continuous work written in two volumes, and the Lukan resurrection narratives are to be found in Luke 24, culminating in Luke 24.50–53:

> Then he led them out as far as Bethany, and lifting up his hands he blessed them. While he blessed them, he parted from them, and was carried up into heaven. And they returned to Jerusalem with great joy, and were continually in the temple blessing God.

Although the reference to the ascension of Jesus, 'was carried up into heaven', is omitted by some of the ancient manuscripts of the Gospel of Luke, modern scholarship in general believes that it was a part of the original text of the gospel. Certainly I myself am fully prepared to argue for its inclusion, and for the consequence, therefore, that it ends the resurrection narratives in Luke–Acts. When the author takes up the story again in Acts 1 he is not interested in the story as a resurrection narrative but rather as the account of a *revelatory discourse* of the risen Lord to his disciples. This is the first example of a literary genre, the revelatory discourse of the risen Lord to his disciples, which became very popular in the ancient church; it is a genre quite distinct from the empty tomb narratives and the appearance stories in the gospels, including those in the Gospel of Luke. I shall not, therefore, discuss it in this book on the resurrection narratives.

In the discussion which follows I shall treat the gospels in the order of Mark, Matthew, and Luke. It is my scholarly conviction that the Gospel of Mark was the first gospel to be written and that it was used as a major source by Matthew and Luke, a conviction shared by the majority of contemporary New Testament scholars. Since this is the consensus opinion of contemporary New Testament scholarship, I will simply accept it and build upon it, without feeling a need to argue the matter itself in any detail – something I would be fully prepared to do. Both Matthew and Luke have used the Gospel of Mark as a source – as they have also used a further common source, a collection of sayings of Jesus commonly referred to as Q (a shorthand expression for the German word *Quelle*, meaning *source*) – but they show absolutely no knowledge of one another's work, and they are generally regarded as having written approximately contemporaneously, but independently of one another. Most scholars would date the Gospel of Mark shortly before or shortly after AD 70, and Matthew and Luke–Acts some twenty years later. I shall discuss Matthew before Luke, not because of any sense of the one's priority over the other, but simply because the narratives in Matthew are rather less complex than those in Luke.

The resurrection narratives as myth

One further point to be made, and a most important one, is that in the discussion that follows I shall have occasion to use the word *myth* in connection with the resurrection narratives, and by implication in connection with other biblical narratives. It is one of the tragedies of the contemporary discussion of biblical texts that the word *myth* has come to carry the negative connotation of something opposed to fact, something not true, such as a 'fairy story' about the gods. The truth is that myths are the narrative expression of the deepest realities of human experience. Myths are ideas people live by, and for which they are prepared to suffer, to kill and be killed. I was born and brought up in England, and I can testify to the force of the myth of the English gentleman, of something being 'simply not cricket'. There have been many occasions when that myth motivated me to one action rather than another, to one decision rather than another, especially during the Second World War. I had the privilege of living for five years in the American South, in Atlanta, Georgia, and I have seen many decisions made and many actions taken, noble and ignoble, on the basis of the myth of 'the South'. Nor have I any doubt but that the enormous effectiveness of the film 'Gone with the Wind' is due in no small part to the instinctive ability of a great actress, Vivien Leigh, to grasp the essence of the myth of the South and to embody it in her unforgettable portrayal of Scarlett O'Hara.

I am penning these lines in Chicago in the early summer of 1976, surrounded on every side by the evidences of the American bicentennial celebration. As a comparatively recent immigrant to this country, I can appreciate the enormous significance of 1776 to the citizens of the USA, even if my British birth makes my feelings a little more mixed than most! The fact is that the millions of immigrants of vastly different ethnic and national backgrounds need a common tradition which will unite them as Americans, so as not simply to perpetuate their separateness as Britishers or Scandinavians, or eastern Europeans, or whatever, who now live in America. This common tradition is found in the events of 1776, and in such symbols of those events as the flag and the Liberty Bell. In the language I like to use, the events of 1776 constitute a myth, a most effective and powerful myth, the myth of American origins, the myth by means of which Americans of diverse ethnic and national backgrounds recognize themselves as having been constituted as a new and distinctive community of human beings. I would call the story of 1776 the foundation myth of American origins, and in saying this I would regard myself as making the strongest and most positive statement I can make about the story. By means of this story, and the subsequent working out of its consequences in the history of the American people, the multitudinous immigrants of diverse origins have created the possibility of a genuine existence in one community *as Americans*.

Although I have called the story of the events of 1776 the foundation myth of American origins, I could just as readily have called it the constitutive history of the American people. For me those would be two ways of saying the same thing; so far as I am concerned *foundation myth* and *constitutive history* – or for that matter *foundation history* and *constitutional myth* – are interchangeable terms. As the story of 1776 comes to be told and retold, as it comes to function as that which constitutes the basis for the life in community of the American people as *Americans*, then clearly the barriers between factual historicity, legendary accretion, and mythical interpretation become blurred. The critical historian will have all kinds of difficulties with the details of the stories because finally, as they function as the means by which the American people regard themselves to be constituted as Americans, these stories are a mixture of history, legend, and myth. They are, if you will, a mixture of mythicized history and historicized myth, but the proportion of one to the other is not relevant to their functioning adequacy as foundation myth or constitutive history.

The matter is no different with regard to the gospel narratives in general or the resurrection narratives in the gospels in particular. The critical historian will determine that they are a mixture of history, legend, and myth, or of mythicized history and historicized myth, and the proportions of one to the other will vary with the findings of the individual historian. But these findings do not affect the functioning adequacy of these narratives as the foundation myth or constitutive history of *Christian origins*. The narratives affirm what it means to say 'Jesus is risen!' and they challenge the reader to accept or to reject the particular understanding of this affirmation which each evangelist has, and the particular vision of the possibilities for life in the world which each evangelist presents. It is the purpose of these chapters to explore each evangelist's understanding of these things in order that the reader today may grasp something of the challenges which Mark, Matthew, and Luke intended when they wrote their narratives so long ago.

As a kind of epilogue to this brief discussion of myth I would like to point to Amos Wilder's listing of various understandings of myth held today, a listing given in his recently published book *Theopoetic: Theology and the Religious Imagination:*

> (1) Myths belong to an outworn mentality and have no meaning for us. (2) Myths are unfortunately still powerful and block a more humane outlook and more humane social patterns. (3) Primordial myths and archetypes constitute the enduring psychic order and orientation of the race. (4) Myths provide the structure of identity and cohesion of particular human groups and ways of life, and are therefore in perpetual conflict with one another. (5) New myths are arising all the time out of new changes in the human situation. (6) By demythologizing, the persisting truth of myth can be identified and reappropriated, as by existential interpretation. (7) Archaic myths can be repossessed even in a rationalistic age by a second level of naiveté (Ricoeur). (8) If the spirits are to be 'tested', so are social dreams and myths which can project man's morbidity as well as his health.

This is a masterly summary of the various understandings of myth which are held today, and just to read it is to understand how difficult it is to use the word *myth* in any discussion of a biblical text. If I discuss a resurrection narrative as myth, and I have every intention of doing that, then the individual reader's reaction to that discussion will depend entirely upon his or her understanding of what the word means. So let me make it quite clear that in this discussion I am using the word with either the third or the fourth of the meanings which Wilder lists. As I discuss the resurrection narratives as myth I mean *either* the sense of 'primordial myths and archetypes' *or* the sense of 'myths [which] provide the structure of identity and cohesion of particular human groups and ways of life'. Moreover, I shall make my meaning clear by referring to the former as *primordial myth* and to the latter as *foundation myth*. Further, as I hope my earlier discussion has made absolutely clear, when I use the word *myth* I am making no judgment about the historicity of the resurrection. The great biblical myths, including that of the resurrection, are like the myth of 1776 in that they are a mixture of mythicized history and historicized myth. The proportions of this mixture are for the critical historian to determine, *if* he or she has the data to make that determination, which in the case of the resurrection narratives he or she does not. But the functioning power of the narrative as myth is not dependent upon any such determination; it is dependent upon the ability of the narrative to resonate with the 'primordial myths and archetypes' of the human race, or to 'provide the structure of identity and cohesion' of a particular human group – in this instance, of Christians.

2

THE RESURRECTION NARRATIVE IN THE GOSPEL OF MARK

The content of the narrative

The first thing we must do is to remind ourselves of the content of the resurrection narrative in the Gospel of Mark. The Gospel of Mark reaches a climax in the death of Jesus and the confession of the centurion (15.37–39):

> And Jesus uttered a loud cry, and breathed his last. And the curtain of the temple was torn in two, from top to bottom. And when the centurion, who stood facing him, saw that he thus breathed his last, he said, 'Truly this man was the Son of God!'

It is the remainder of the narrative of the Gospel of Mark which concerns us, for we now find a complex of three closely related narratives (15.40–41; 15.42–47; 16.1–8), all of which emphasize the role of a group of women, and which must be considered as one continuous unit. They read as follows:

Part One – The Women at the Cross (15.40–41):

> There were also women looking on from afar, among whom were Mary Magdalene, and Mary the mother of James the younger and of Joses, and Salome, who when he was in Galilee, followed him, and ministered to him: and also many other women who came up with him to Jerusalem.

Part Two – The Women at the Burial (15.42–47):

> And when evening had come, since it was the day of Preparation, that is, the day before the sabbath, Joseph of Arimathea, a respected member of the council, who was also himself looking for the kingdom of God, took courage and went to Pilate, and asked for the body of Jesus. And Pilate wondered if he were already dead: and summoning the centurion, he asked him if he was already dead. And when he learned from the centurion

> that he was dead, he granted the body to Joseph. And he bought a linen shroud, and taking him down, wrapped him in the linen shroud, and laid him in a tomb which had been hewn out of the rock; and he rolled a stone against the door of the tomb. Mary Magdalene and Mary the mother of Joses saw where he was laid.

Part Three – The Women at the Empty Tomb (16.1–8):

> And when the sabbath was past, Mary Magdalene, and Mary the mother of James, and Salome, bought spices, so that they might go and anoint him. And very early on the first day of the week they went to the tomb when the sun had risen. And they were saying to one another, 'Who will roll away the stone for us from the door of the tomb?' And looking up, they saw that the stone was rolled back – it was very large. And entering the tomb, they saw a young man sitting on the right side, dressed in a white robe; and they were amazed. And he said to them, 'Do not be amazed; you seek Jesus of Nazareth, who was crucified. He has risen, he is not here; see the place where they laid him. But . . . he is going before you to Galilee; there you will see him, as he told you.' And they went out and fled from the tomb; for trembling and astonishment had come upon them; and they said nothing to any one, for they were afraid.

The ending of the gospel

In considering this three-part narrative the first thing to be determined is whether this is the narrative which originally ended the Gospel of Mark. Did the gospel as the evangelist himself originally composed it end on this enigmatic note, the women saying nothing to anyone because they were afraid, or did it go on to say something further, something which was subsequently either lost or suppressed? This is a very important question indeed, and we cannot begin to discuss the resurrection narrative in the Gospel of Mark without first attempting to determine where that narrative originally ended. There are three factors to be taken into account in considering this question: (1) the evidence of the ancient manuscripts, (2) the fact that as it stands Mark 16.8 ends with a conjunction, and (3) the physical possibilities with regard to the accidental or deliberate mutilation of the original text of the gospel. We will consider each of these factors in turn.

(1) The evidence of the ancient manuscripts is clear: the only text of the gospel which ever began to circulate in the ancient world ended with the reference to the fear of the women in what is now Mark 16.8. Matthew and Luke, who based their own work on the Gospel of Mark, both worked from a text of the gospel which ended at 16.8. It is the virtually unanimous opinion of modern scholarship that what appears in most translations of the gospel as Mark 16.9–20 is a pastiche of material taken from the other gospels and added to the original text of the gospel as it was copied and transmitted by the scribes of the ancient Christian communities. All the evidence indicates that every manuscript of the gospel which we now have or of which we have any knowledge, is ultimately descended from a manuscript which ended at 16.8.

(2) Mark 16.8 in the original Greek ends with the phrase *ephobounto gar*, 'for they were afraid', and *gar* is a conjunction. Now it is as grammatically barbarous to end a sentence with a conjunction in ancient Greek as it is to end one with a preposition in modern English, and there is no other known example from ancient Greek literature of a whole book ending with a conjunction. This consideration alone is sufficient to convince many scholars that the original text of the gospel cannot have ended at 16.8; that there must have been either an accidental or deliberate mutilation of whatever it was that originally followed the conjunction *gar*. But I feel that this consideration is not as strong as it might appear. I was myself taught most strictly never to end sentences with prepositions – nor for that matter ever to split an infinitive. But today I have friends and colleagues who would not give a second thought to either ending a sentence with a preposition or splitting an infinitive, so I would recognize and argue that the rules of the ancient Greek grammarians are not necessarily binding upon the

evangelist Mark. As a matter of fact, the Greek which Mark writes often has the kind of vividness and simplicity that one associates with the teller of folk tales, but there are also things about it for which he would have had his knuckles rapped in a classroom where Greek rhetoric was taught! So although the *ephobounto gar* with which Mark 16.8 ends is grammatically a barbarism, it is nonetheless possible that the evangelist could have ended his work in this way.

(3) The physical possibilities with regard to the accidental or deliberate mutilation of the original text of the gospel are not difficult to assess. It is very difficult indeed to think of circumstances under which an accidental mutilation would not have been repaired, or under which a deliberate mutilation and hence successful suppression of the original ending could have been carried out. In this connection, I must repeat my earlier statement that, so far as we know, every early copy of the gospel which circulated ended at 16.8. Now the Gospel of Mark was a very successful early Christian document. It circulated rapidly and widely; within a generation it was being used and reinterpreted in Christian communities which were as different from one another as were those communities represented by the evangelists Matthew and Luke, and in my view the evangelist John also shows that he knows it. Since all of these early copies ended at 16.8 this means that if there was a mutilation, accidental or deliberate, it must have been a mutilation of the autograph copy, or of an early copy of the autograph copy from which all subsequent copies were made. It is very difficult to conceive of circumstances under which the author, or one of his followers, would not have repaired an accidental mutilation. In the circumstances of the Christian communities shortly after AD 70 it is equally difficult to think of anyone with the authority to carry out a deliberate mutilation and successful suppression of an original ending.

The absence of appearance stories

I have argued carefully this point about the Gospel of Mark ending intentionally at 16.8, because it is a most important point. If the gospel originally ended at 16.8 then it never included any *appearance stories* – stories of the risen Jesus appearing to his disciples. But if that is the case, then the evangelist Mark has an understanding of the resurrection of Jesus radically different from that represented by the apostle Paul, who recounts a list of appearances (I Cor. 15.5–7), or by the other evangelists, all of whom offer appearance stories. This matter is so important that we must ask ourselves whether there are any other factors we can consider, factors other than the intrinsic probability of the ending being at 16.8. Fortunately there are three such factors to be considered: (1) the interpretation of the passion of Jesus presented by Mark earlier in his gospel, (2) the references to 'going before you into Galilee' in 14.28 and 16.7, and (3) the roles of the disciples and the women in the story of the ministry of Jesus as Mark presents it. We will consider each of these factors in turn, the first in considerable detail, and as we do so we shall find ourselves moving closer to an understanding of Mark's theology of the resurrection.

(1) The passion of Jesus

It is a fact well recognized by interpreters of the Gospel of Mark that the long central section of the gospel is concerned to present Mark's own understanding of the passion of Jesus, of the necessity for and significance of Jesus' death, and of the nature and meaning of the resurrection. The section is set off by two giving-of-sight stories, stories of Jesus giving sight to a blind man at Bethsaida (8.22–26) and blind Bartimaeus at Jericho (10.46–52). These stories are symbolic of the power of Jesus to give sight to the blind – they are the only two such stories in the Gospel of Mark – and they offset and highlight the central section of the gospel (8.27–10.45), in which Jesus attempts to give 'sight' to his disciples, that is, attempts to teach them the meaning of his impending passion. But in this he fails. The Jesus who could give sight to the physically blind could not give insight and understanding to the disciples. For Mark this is one of the great tragic motifs of the gospel story, and as he tells the story he is constantly reaching out beyond the disciples to his own readers, attempting to get them to understand what the disciples had so significantly failed to understand.

Mark does this by means of three carefully constructed 'prediction units', units of narrative which follow a consistent pattern: (*a*) prediction by Jesus of his passion; (*b*) misunderstanding by the disciples, and (*c*) teaching by Jesus in an attempt to correct the misunderstanding.

(*a*) *The prediction units*. These are as follows:

prediction	8.31	9.31	10.33–34
misunderstanding	8:32–33	9.32	10.35–41
teaching	8.34–9.1	9.33–37	10.42–45

The last section of teaching concludes, as one would expect, with the climactic interpretation of the cross: 'The Son of man also came not to be served but to serve, and to give his life as a ransom for many.' But it is the passion predictions themselves that concern us most closely, and so we turn to look at them in some detail. In the Revised Standard Version they read as follows (italics mine):

8.31 And he began to teach them
that the Son of man must suffer many things
and be rejected by the elders and the chief priests and the scribes,
and be killed,
and after three days rise again.

9.31 'The Son of man will be delivered into the hands of men,
and they will kill him;
and when he is killed, after three days he will rise.'

10.33–34 'Behold we are going up to Jerusalem:
and the Son of man will be delivered to the chief priests and the scribes,
and they will condemn him to death, and deliver him to the Gentiles;
and they will mock him, and spit upon him, and scourge him and kill him;
and after three days he will rise.'

As one considers these three predictions together two things become immediately obvious: the variations in the references to the passion, and the stereotyped lack of variation in the references to the resurrection.

The references to the passion vary between the two distinctive ways of referring to the passion of Jesus in the New Testament traditions. The first uses the Greek verb *dei* ('must'), which is often used to designate divine necessity, especially the divine necessity revealed in scripture (for example, Mark 9.11; 13.7; Acts 1.16); the second and third references use the Greek verb *paradidonai* ('to deliver up'), which is used in the New Testament as a technical term to describe the passion of Jesus, especially in I Cor. 11.23, where 'on the night when he was betrayed' (= 'was delivered up') virtually means 'on the night when the passion began'. Mark himself is particularly fond of the latter verb. He uses it in connection with the fate of John the Baptist in 1.14 ('after John was arrested' [= 'delivered up']), in connection with the fate of Jesus in the second and third passion predictions, and in connection with the potential fate of Christian martyrs in 13.9 ('they will deliver you up to councils'). By using this verb in this way Mark makes it quite clear that he sees a striking element of equivalence in the fates of John the Baptist, of Jesus, and of the early Christian martyrs: all alike are 'delivered up'; at the level of theological meaning, each alike suffers a 'passion'. This is a very striking insight, and since it is Mark's own it is not surprising that he uses the verb *paradidonai* in two of his three passion predictions.

The evangelist Mark is very fond of threefold repetitions,

and he is also very fond of minor variations within the repetitions. So there are three passion predictions: one using *dei*, two using *paradidonai*. Similarly, there are three references to the women after the centurion's confession in 15.39; and there is a similar variation. At the cross it is 'Mary Magdalene, and Mary the mother of James the younger and of Joses, and Salome' (15.40). At the burial it is 'Mary Magdalene and Mary the mother of Joses' (15.47), while at the empty tomb it is 'Mary Magdalene, and Mary the mother of James, and Salome' (16.1). These references to the women do not carry the theological weight of the use of *dei* and *paradidonai* in the passion predictions, but they do testify to Mark's fondness for threefold repetition, and for variation within the repetitions. They also indicate that he has had a considerable hand in shaping the final literary form of the narrative about the women, as indeed he has had a considerable hand in shaping the final literary form of the passion predictions. This is an important point to note because it means that both in the narrative about the women and in the passion predictions Mark's own theological concerns will be close to the surface.

The variations in the passion predictions go beyond the use of *dei* and *paradidonai*. The first and third offer considerable detail concerning the passion itself; indeed the third is almost a summary of the events of chapters 14 and 15 of the gospel. The second, on the other hand, is terse to the point of being brusque: 'The Son of man will be delivered . . . and they will kill him; and when he is killed . . .' These variations in the references to the passion serve to highlight the stereotyped nature of the references to the resurrection in these predictions: '. . . after three days rise again', '. . . after three days he will rise', '. . . after three days he will rise'. Here the references are always terse; the verb is always the same (*anistanai*); and we have the uniform 'after three days'. This last point is particularly interesting in that early Christian tradition normally uses 'on the third day' in such references, as at I Cor. 15.4. As a matter of fact, both Matthew and Luke change Mark's reference to 'on the third day' (Matt. 16.21 ‖ Mark 8.31 ‖ Luke 9.22; Matt. 17.23 ‖ Mark 9.31 [Luke 9.44 omits the reference]; Matt. 20.19 ‖ Mark 10.34 ‖ Luke 18.33). So it is immediately apparent that these terse references to the resurrection, with their characteristic '*after* three days', are very important to Mark himself.

The uniformly terse nature of these references to the resurrection is in startling contrast to the fullness of the references to the passion in the first and third predictions. Clearly Mark is not nearly so interested in the details of the resurrection as he is in those of the passion, and this fact strengthens our suspicion that the absence of resurrection appearance stories from the gospel is the consequence of a deliberate choice by the evangelist to omit any such stories from his narrative. Mark is not concerned with the resurrection in and of itself; he is concerned with it as the essential prelude to something else. What is that 'something else'? I suggest that it is, first, the immediate state of Jesus after the resurrection, a state symbolized by the story of the transfiguration, and that it is, secondly, the parousia, which comes to great prominence towards the end of the gospel – for example, in chapter 13 and in the reply to the high priest in 14.62.

The symbolic significance of the transfiguration narrative. The state of Jesus after his resurrection is represented by the transfiguration narrative (Mark 9.2–8), which Mark links to the passion predictions in a quite remarkable manner. The transfiguration narrative begins, 'And after six days . . . ', and this is the only place in the narrative of the gospel, prior to the passion narrative itself, where one finds such an exact reference. Mark normally says 'in those days', 'in the morning', 'one sabbath', and the like. The only other place in the gospel narrative where one finds anything like this is in the passion predictions with their uniform and remarkable 'after three days' with reference to the resurrection. It is impossible to resist the conclusion that these two references are related; that the 'after six days' of the transfiguration deliberately picks up the 'after three days' of the resurrection references; that the evangelist is deliberately linking the transfiguration narrative to the resurrection references in order to say something to his readers. This conclusion becomes even more certain when we notice Mark 9.9: 'And as they were coming down the mountain [i.e., from the transfiguration], he charged them to tell no one what they had seen, until the Son of man should have risen from the dead.' In other words, the transfiguration becomes important *after* the resurrection; it is symbolic of the post-resurrection situation.

The next step is to recognize that Mark and his readers both thought of Moses and Elijah as being already with God in the heavens. It was uniformly held that God had taken Moses to be with him in the heavens, and there is an apocalyptic work from the period which is based on this conviction, *The Assumption of Moses*. That Elijah was already with God in the heavens was taught in I Kings 2.1–10, an account of Elijah being taken into heaven by a whirlwind. So when Jesus is seen in a transfigured state speaking with Moses and Elijah, he is being seen proleptically in his post-resurrection state and situation: he is in heaven with Moses and Elijah awaiting the moment of his return to earth as Son of man.

Mark's emphasis on the parousia. That Mark anticipated the return to earth of Jesus as Son of man, the parousia, and that he anticipated this as imminent – that this is indeed a major theme of his gospel – is so well known and widely accepted that I need not argue the point in detail. I will mention only three things. First, the first prediction unit comes to a climax in the promise of the parousia. In 9.1 we read, 'There are some standing here who will not taste death before they see the kingdom of God come with power' (Jerusalem Bible; the Revised Standard Version's 'has come' is somewhat tendentious). Then, secondly, chapter 13 is solely concerned with the scenario for the coming of the Son of man and the urgent need for the reader to prepare himself for that coming. Finally, it is the main emphasis in the reply of Jesus to the high priest in 14.62: 'I am; and you will see the Son of man seated at the right hand of power, and coming with the clouds of heaven.' Indeed, that saying envisages the whole post-resurrection situation of Jesus: 'seated at the right hand of power', that is, with God in the heavens, and 'coming with the clouds of heaven' at the parousia.

(2) Galilee

In Mark 14.28 Jesus tells his disciples, 'After I am raised up I will go before you into Galilee', and in 16.7 the young man at the empty tomb repeats this message: 'He is going before you into Galilee; there you will see him, as he told you.' Now the question is, What did *Mark* understand and intend by these references to Galilee? As we shall see later, *Matthew* understood them as references to a resurrection appearance of Jesus to his disciples, and as a consequence of this he locates the climactic resurrection appearance of Jesus in Galilee. But it seems extremely unlikely that *Mark* understood the reference in this way. For Mark, geographical references are always heavily symbolic, and a group of British scholars (R. H. Lightfoot, G. H. Boobyer, and C. F. Evans) have shown that references to Galilee in the gospel are primarily references to the Gentile mission of the early Christian church. When Mark speaks of Jesus preaching and teaching in Galilee he is symbolizing the mission of the early Christian church, in the name of Jesus, to the Gentile world. This symbolic use of geographical references to Galilee means that the narrative of the Gospel of Mark is always moving at two different levels. On the one hand it moves at the historical level of the physical/geographical references to Jesus in Galilee, while on the other hand it moves at the symbolic level of a series of references to the experience of Christians, in the name of Jesus, in the Gentile world. These two levels at which the narrative of the gospel moves are extremely difficult to sort out, and there is the obvious danger of assuming either that too much is symbolic or that too much is historical/physical/geographical.

In the case of the references to 'going before you into Galilee' in 14.28 and 16.7, however, the symbolic reference seems the more natural. The references are to a post-resurrection situation; 'after I am raised up' in 14.28 and the empty tomb in 16.7 make that quite clear. In a post-resurrection situation a symbolic reference is the more natural, and these references may be taken to be references to Jesus leading his disciples into the Gentile world. It is in the Gentile world of the church's mission that they will see him. Of course, they could still 'see him' in a resurrection appearance or in a vision like that of Paul on the Damascus road, but in view of the juxtaposition of the passion predictions and the transfiguration, the reader would most naturally think of the reference as being to the parousia.

(3) The disciples and the women

The role of the disciples in the Gospel of Mark is a very important one. The first act of the ministry in Galilee is that of Jesus calling disciples (1.16–20), and disciples are constantly with Jesus throughout that ministry. In 3.13–19 Jesus formally appoints the Twelve, whom Mark carefully names, and in 6.7–13 he sends them out on a mission on his behalf. After their return from this mission the disciples begin to figure even more prominently in the narrative, but with a change in that they are now depicted as failing in understanding. In 6.52 'they did not understand about the loaves . . . their hearts were hardened', and in 8.15–21 Jesus has occasion to enter into a dialogue with them about their failure to understand. In the long central interpretative section of the gospel this failing in understanding becomes more acute as the disciples misunderstand each of the three predictions of the passion. We noted above how Mark presents these misunderstandings schematically at 8.32–33, 9.32, and 10.35–41. More than that, in this section also the disciples are depicted as losing the ability to cast out demons, a power they had possessed since their appointment (9.14–29). So they are now being depicted as failing both in understanding and in power.

As the story of Jesus and his fate moves to Jerusalem and the passion narrative, the depiction of the disciples' failure escalates, for now they are shown as failing in loyalty also. At the Last Supper Jesus predicts his betrayal by a disciple (14.18–21), and on the Mount of Olives he further predicts, 'You will all fall away; for it is written, "I will strike the shepherd and the sheep will be scattered".' And when Peter protests his loyalty, Jesus says to him, 'This very night, before the cock crows twice, you will deny me three times' (14.26–31). In the following narratives these predictions are dramatically fulfilled. At Gethsemane Peter, James, and John fail to keep watch with Jesus (14.32–42); at the betrayal and arrest of Jesus, 'they all forsook him, and fled' (14.50); and while Jesus is on trial before the Sanhedrin Peter denies him three times, formally and with oaths (14.66–72).

After their flight from the arrest the disciples disappear from the narrative of the Gospel of Mark, except for Peter, who similarly disappears after his denial of Jesus. The only further reference to them at all is in the words of the young man at the tomb to the women, 'Go, tell his disciples and Peter . . .' (16.7). At his cross Jesus is surrounded by strangers, and in an ultimate act of irony he is confessed as Son of God in his death not by a disciple but by the centurion responsible for his execution (15.39).

Now it is precisely at this point that the women appear in the narrative, for the three-point narrative concerning the women at the cross, the burial, and the empty tomb begins immediately following the centurion's confession, as I pointed out at the beginning of this chapter. From this point the women take over the role in the gospel narrative which one might have expected to be played by the disciples. After the death of Jesus they provide the element of continuity as they move to their climactic discovery of the empty tomb. Moreover Mark himself has already warned his readers of the importance of the story of the attempt to anoint the body of Jesus, with which the passion narrative ends, through his introduction of the passion narrative by means of the story of the anointing of Jesus by the woman at Bethany. It is a literary characteristic of Mark that he frames large sections of his narrative with related stories which serve to interpret that narrative to the reader. So he begins the first major section of his gospel with the first miracle story, the exorcism at Capernaum (1.21–28), and ends it with the miracle-failure story, the rejection of Jesus in 'his own country' (6.1–6). He frames the next major section of the gospel by means of the two feeding stories (6.31–44; 8.1–9). Then the central section of the gospel is framed by the two giving-of-sight stories (8.22–26; 10.46–52), as we have already noted. Now the passion narrative is framed by the two anointing stories, and the one serves to call attention to the other. Mark is telling his readers that the body of Jesus had to be anointed 'beforehand for burying' because the resurrection would make a later anointing impossible, as indeed it does.

We are now almost in a position to begin a direct discussion of Mark's understanding of the resurrection of Jesus, but before we do that there is one last point to be made about the women and their role in the Markan narrative as compared to that of the disciples: like the disciples, the women also fail their master. Unlike the disciples the women stay faithful to Jesus to the extent of 'looking on from afar' at the cross, and being prepared to play their role in anointing Jesus. Hence it is their great honour to discover the empty tomb and the fact of the resurrection. But it is precisely at this point that the women, like the disciples before them, fail their trust. They are entrusted with the message to the disciples and Peter, but 'they said nothing to any one, for they were afraid'. In the Gospel of Mark the discipleship failure is total. The disciples forsake Jesus as a group and flee from the arrest; Peter denies him with oaths while he is on trial; the women, who take on the role of the disciples in this final three-part narrative, fail to deliver the message entrusted to them.

We are so used to reading Mark in the light of Matthew and Luke, where the women do deliver the message, that it is difficult for us to appreciate the sheer, stark force of the Markan narrative. In Mark every disciple fails the master; every intimate sooner or later fails him in one way or another. It is the centurion who finally understands him, and a sympathetic outsider who buries him. The disciples, Peter, the women – these all ultimately fail their responsibility and trust. It would take us too far afield to discuss why Mark paints this grim picture. It is obviously part of his overall understanding of the true nature and possibilities of Christian discipleship; and equally obviously Mark's narrative moves at both the historical and symbolic levels. The disciples and the women are at one and the same time the historical figures – Peter, the others and Mary Magdalene – and symbolic figures representing the possibilities and actualities of discipleship in the Christian communities which Mark knows and for which he writes.

A discussion of Mark's understanding of discipleship is quite beyond the scope of this present work, which is concerned with Mark's understanding of the resurrection of Jesus. But there is one aspect of the discipleship theme which is important to the resurrection theme, and that is that the totality of discipleship failure in Mark reinforces the contention that there never were any resurrection appearance stories in the gospel. An appearance of the risen Lord to a disciple, or one to the women, necessarily implies an element of restitution, of renewal of trust and confidence, and Mark's vision of discipleship failure is too stark for that. What Mark sees in 14.28 and 16.7 is not restitution and a renewal of trust through a resurrection appearance but the judgment of the imminent parousia. By reading Mark in the light of Matthew and Luke we have failed to do justice to the dark side of his particular vision.

Summary

It will be evident by now that for me the resurrection narrative in Mark is the threefold narrative concerning the women at the cross, the burial, and the empty tomb. We cannot treat 16.1–8 separately from 15.40–41 and 15.42–47, because it is those first two elements in the three-part narrative which identify for us the women and their role in the narrative as a whole. Moreover we must also be careful to remember the story of the anointing at Bethany, which together with its counterpart, the failure to anoint the body at the tomb, frames and interprets the passion narrative as a whole. But I have already discussed those things at some length, so I may now proceed in a more summary fashion.

On this whole matter I must now simply rest my case and leave it to my own readers to judge whether or not my arguments are convincing. For my part I will turn to Mark's understanding of the resurrection of Jesus as it appears if we assume that the gospel always ended at 16.8. The crux of the matter here is the careful juxtaposition of the transfiguration 'after six days' with the 'after three days' of the stereotyped references to the resurrection in the passion predictions. What Mark is doing here is telling his readers what it means for him to say that God has raised Jesus from the dead: it means that God has vindicated Jesus out of his death and taken him into the heavens to be with Moses and Elijah until the moment, the imminent moment, of his parousia. Hence the body that had to be anointed beforehand; hence the empty tomb; hence the references to Jesus 'going before you' to symbolic Galilee, references to the parousia. Hence also the lack of appearance stories, for appearance stories imply a new state of things *between* the resurrection and the parousia, as we shall see when we come to discuss Matthew and Luke. But for Mark the only state of things between the resurrection and the parousia is that brief interim period in which Christians learn the meaning of true discipleship, and accept the reality of their own suffering as they learn to appreciate the meaning of their Master's, all in anticipation of the judgment and glory of the parousia.

Mark writes his gospel to express the conviction that Jesus is the Christ, the Son of God. This christological theme he pursues all the way from the superscription to the whole work in 1.1, 'The beginning of the gospel of Jesus Christ, the Son of God', to the climactic confession of the centurion at the cross in 15.39, 'Truly this man was the Son of God.' But Mark is also concerned to express the conviction that it was necessary for the Son of God to suffer and die; that he suffered and died as the Son of God and Son of man; that God vindicated him out of his death as Son of man and took him to be with Moses and Elijah in the heavens to await the imminence of his parousia in 'Galilee' as Son of God. It is this element of the Markan concern that reaches its climax in the resurrection narrative and which until now we have therefore been pursuing. There is also a further element in the Markan concern, and that is the theme of discipleship. In this connection I have pursued only the element of discipleship failure, because that is a major element in the resurrection narratives. The theme as a whole must await discussion on another occasion.

The Markan resurrection narrative as myth

The Markan resurrection narrative is to be understood as myth, but it is to be understood as primordial myth rather than as foundation myth. In stark contrast to Matthew and Luke, Mark is not concerned with the founding of a Christian community as distinct from the Jewish community. He is concerned with all men and women everywhere as they face the imminent parousia of the Son of man. So he strikes the primordial theme of suffering/death/the overcoming of death. That this is a primordial theme is evident; evidences of it are found everywhere in human culture. In this connection the discussion of the gospel of Mark in *Kerygma and Comedy in the New Testament* by Dan O. Via, Jr, is particularly interesting. Via is able to show how thoroughly impregnated with this theme the Gospel of Mark is – although Via uses structuralist terminology and calls it a 'deep, generative structure of the human mind' rather than a 'primordial theme'. But that is only a terminological distinction. The fact is that the theme of suffering/death/overcoming of death dominates the Gospel of Mark. Mark sees it in the suffering/death/overcoming of death in resurrection in the case of Jesus; he sees it in the prospective suffering/death/overcoming of death at the parousia in the case of the believer. This is his fundamental and over-riding concern, and it is this which leads him to his particular understanding of the resurrection.

The women are surrogate figures for the disciples, who have disappeared from the narrative as a consequence of their failure as disciples. So the women become Jesus' comparative intimates, to whom the announcement of the resurrection makes sense because they have the general context of knowledge of the story of Jesus and his ministry in which to set it. In accordance with Mark's own dark vision of discipleship failure the women, too, fail their trust, but they have served their narrative function of establishing, for the reader of the gospel, the fact of the resurrection of Jesus. We must always remember that Mark writes specifically for readers and that his narratives, therefore, move at several different levels. Not only do they move at the historical and the symbolic levels to which I have several times called attention, they also move at the level of the reader, and the reader knows in general that Jesus is Son of God; he or she knows how the story 'came out'. So Mark can assume things about his readers and gear his own narratives accordingly.

Now the Gospel of Mark was written within a Christian community for the use of that community, and one of the things that Mark could assume about his readers would be a general acceptance of Jesus as risen from the dead, and some kind of awareness of resurrection appearance stories. When Mark therefore establishes the resurrection of Jesus by means of the third element in his narrative concerning the women, he is striking chords in the minds of his readers, many of whom could be reading his gospel *because* they believed that God had raised Jesus from the dead. But when he goes on *not* to narrate an appearance story he is contradicting every expectation his readers would have held concerning the natural continuation of the story. He is also making an extremely strong statement about his own understanding of what it means to say that God has raised Jesus from the dead. It is for this reason that I have been at pains to argue that the Gospel of Mark never did include an appearance story, that it always ended at 16.8 with the failure of the women – despite Matthew and Luke, who promptly added appearance stories; despite the scribes of the ancient church who added appearance stories to their texts of the gospel, giving us the current passage 16.9–20; and despite modern scholarship with its theories of accidental or deliberate mutilation. It is my contention that the gospel always did end at 16.8, because with the failure of the women the story which Mark set out to tell reached its proper ending.

Another consequence of the dominance of this primordial theme for Mark is his presentation of discipleship failure. His concern is for archetypal absolutes, for the clash of ultimacies, so everything is painted in the starkest possible colours. So, in Mark's vision, Jesus is totally abandoned by his disciples; just as Jesus in his death is totally abandoned by God: 'My God, my God, why hast thou forsaken me?' (Mark 15.34). Similarly the victory at the parousia will be a total victory. Jesus says,

> 'But in those days, after that tribulation, the sun will be darkened, and the moon will not give its light, and the stars will be falling from heaven, and the powers in the heavens will be shaken. And then they will see the Son of Man coming in clouds with great power and glory. And then he will send out the angels and gather his elect from the four winds, from the ends of the earth to the ends of heaven' (Mark 13.24–27).

For me the Gospel of Mark is the gospel which comes closest to the primordial element in great art. It is perhaps not inappropriate to add that I am writing these lines to the accompaniment of Prokofiev's *Romeo and Juliet*; I have tried writing to the accompaniment of Stravinsky's *Rite of Spring*, but that proved *too* primordial! Mark takes the elements of the gospel story and weaves them together in a literary composition which brings out the primordial themes inherent in that story. His gospel resonates in particular with the theme of suffering/death/overcoming of death, and, for Mark, to say 'Jesus is risen!' is to resonate with that theme.

The interpretation of the Markan resurrection narrative

This section is somewhat difficult to write because there is a sense in which one cannot offer verbal interpretations of primordial themes; one either responds to and resonates with them or one does not. In a sense I can no more interpret the Markan resurrection narrative than I can interpret Prokofiev's *Romeo and Juliet* or Stravinsky's *Rite of Spring*. What I can do, and what I have done, is to attempt to show how the narrative came to be written as it is written, what has gone into it, and how other parts of the work as a whole relate to it and help us to understand it, which is what the music critic would do with the final part of the Prokofiev or the Stravinsky. This is what I have done here in my capacity as a New Testament scholar. But obviously there is a challenge to attempt more than that, a challenge to go on to interpret the narrative into the present – into my present and into the present of my readers. To this challenge I shall now attempt to respond, but I want to make it clear that I no longer regard myself as speaking with the authority of a New Testament scholar. I am simply expressing the convictions of one to whom the Markan narrative is meaningful.

The Markan narrative is essentially primordial myth, and it is dominated by the imminent parousia, the imminent coming of Jesus as Son of man as apocalyptic judge and redeemer. It is extremely difficult to offer a verbal interpretation of the primordial theme, but the parousia is a different matter. I will turn, therefore, to the parousia.

In a recently published book, *Jesus and the Language of the Kingdom*, I argued that in the message of Jesus, 'Kingdom of God' was a *tensive* symbol (the term is from Philip Wheelwright's *Metaphor and Reality*), that is, it is a symbol which is not exhausted by any one referent but which can have a series of related referents. Since that is the case, then when Jesus spoke of the coming of the kingdom he was not referring to one eschatological event which all people everywhere would experience at the same time. Rather he was referring to an event which each person would experience in his or her own time. He was referring to the experience of God as King which each person experiences in terms of the concrete actuality of his or her own life. He was speaking of the experience of ultimacy in the historicality of the every-day. I can only state that conclusion here, referring the reader to the above-mentioned book itself for detailed argument and exegesis.

This understanding of what it means to speak of the coming of the kingdom of God did not persist in the early Christian communities. The early Christian communities were dominated by apocalyptic expectation, and they lacked the sovereign ability of Jesus of Nazareth to shatter and to reshape the categories of the language being used. Early apocalyptic Christianity interpreted the coming of the kingdom in terms of the coming of Jesus himself as Son of man, as in Luke 17.20–36, and insofar as they expected the coming of the Son of man, the parousia, at a concrete point in calendar time, as Mark certainly did, they transformed the tensive symbol into a *steno*-symbol. A steno-symbol (again the term is Wheelwright's) is a symbol which is exhausted in one referent and which can have no further referent. This linguistic shift changes everything, and the expectation which Jesus had is transformed into a new and very different one. Now the kingdom comes in the form of Jesus as Son of man, and it comes to all people everywhere at the same time. Now it is no longer a matter of the experience of ultimacy in the historicality of the every-day, but of the destruction of every-dayness itself and its replacement by something entirely different.

But in speaking of the coming of the Son of man we do not *have* to use 'Son of man' as a steno-symbol. Admittedly

Mark himself does, but in view of the linguistic shift from Jesus to early apocalyptic Christianity we may surely reverse the process and interpret 'Son of man' as a tensive symbol, interpreting 'coming of the Son of man' as Jesus himself interpreted 'coming of the kingdom of God'. We may again speak of the experience of ultimacy in the historicality of the every-day, only now we define that ultimacy in terms of the Jesus of the gospel story, and in terms of the Jesus of the Markan primordial myth.

I may summarize my interpretation of the Markan resurrection narrative in one sentence. For me to say 'Jesus is risen' in Markan terms means to say that I experience Jesus as ultimacy in the historicality of my every-day, and that that experience transforms my every-dayness as Mark expected the coming of Jesus as Son of man to transform the world.

3

THE RESURRECTION NARRATIVES IN THE GOSPEL OF MATTHEW

Redaction criticism as a tool in interpretation

In the case of the gospels of Matthew and Luke we have an important interpretative tool that we can use, one which makes the work of interpretation both somewhat simpler and somewhat more sure than it is in the case of the Gospel of Mark. This tool is the method of redaction criticism. It is a literary fact that both Matthew and Luke used the Gospel of Mark as a major source, basing large sections of their own work upon it. Since we have the Gospel of Mark ourselves we can observe the changes they make, and the additions they introduce; we can observe the way they edit the text of Mark as they use that text as a source. The technical term for such an editorial process in German is *Redaktion* (in English, *redaction*); hence *redaction criticism* is the technical term for our careful observation of it.

It turns out that a careful observation of Matthew's or Luke's redaction of the Gospel of Mark gives us important insights into their particular theological motivation. We find that there are both consistent trends in their redaction and spectacular singular instances of it. Almost invariably we find that both the consistent trends and the singular instances represent a change in the understanding of the significance of Jesus and his story for the Christian believer; in other words, the redaction is theologically motivated. Now the observation of redaction is something that can be checked and verified, and the argument from redaction to theological motivation is something that has to satisfy the canons of reasonable argument. This means that quite suddenly the interpreters of the gospels of Matthew and Luke have in their hands an interpretative method that is, as it were, publicly available, a method that offers both an objective starting point and the reasonable expectation of a consensus agreement as to results among the competent scholars. It is for this reason that redaction criticism has become so important in the interpretation of the gospels of Matthew and Luke, and today it is the usual starting point for the work of the interpreter of those gospels. I should perhaps emphasize the phrase *starting point* in that last sentence. No interpreter of the gospels could hope to be successful who limited himself or herself to one interpretative method, however promising, and today most interpreters would insist on the use of both historical criticism and a more general literary criticism, in addition to the more specialized redaction criticism, as they set about the task of interpretation. But redaction criticism is the starting point, so let us begin our discussion of the resurrection narratives in Matthew by observing Matthew's redaction of the Markan narrative.

Matthew's redaction of the Markan narrative concerning the women

Matthew 27.55–56 is Matthew's version of the women at the cross, and the redactional element here is minimal. The only real change is that in the list of women Matthew substitutes 'the mother of the sons of Zebedee' for Mark's 'Salome'. Whatever the reason may be for this change, it is not theologically significant.

Matthew's version of the story of the women at the burial comes at 27.57–61. In it there is one significant redactional change in that Joseph of Arimathea is identified as 'a disciple of Jesus'. This is part of a distinctive trend in Matthew's redaction: he does not share Mark's dark vision of discipleship failure and he consistently presents the disciples in a better light than does Mark. I will give some examples of this. Matthew omits the reference to the disciples' lack of understanding in Mark 6.52, and the dialogue about their misunderstanding is considerably milder in Matthew 16.5–12 than it was in Mark 8.14–21. Again the reference to misunderstanding is omitted from the second passion prediction (Matt. 17.22–23 || Mark 9.30–32). Even where such references are retained, they are sometimes given an interesting ecclesiastical ring, that is, they symbolize comparative lack of faith among members of the early Christian church. This is the case with the stilling of the storm (Matt. 8.23–27 || Mark 4.35–41), and with the disciples' loss of power (Matt. 17.14–21 || Mark 9.14–19). In both instances Matthew introduces the ecclesiastical term *little faith*, and by means of this and other redactional changes he turns Mark's stories of discipleship failure into allegories of the state of the church in his own day. Of course Mark himself constantly moves between the historical level of Jesus and his disciples and the symbolic level of the Christian communities of his own day, as I pointed out, but he always maintains a dynamic tension between the two levels. But in some of the stories in Matthew, perhaps especially in these two, this tension is lost. The historical level is now simply a vehicle for the symbolic: the stories have become allegories. In the passion narrative Matthew maintains Mark's references to discipleship failure – the Gethsemane scene, the flight of the disciples at the arrest of Jesus, Peter's denial – but then he mellows the Markan starkness by making Joseph of Arimathea a disciple rather than the sympathetic stranger he is in Mark.

I have given these details of Matthew's treatment of the Markan theme of discipleship failure because it is a good example of the way in which redaction criticism works. We noted that Matthew is concerned to present the disciples in a better light than does Mark, that he can and does turn some of the stories into allegories of the church of his own day, and that he mellows the Markan theme of discipleship failure. From these few observations we have learnt a good deal about Matthew's characteristic concerns, and Mark's characteristic concerns have been highlighted by the contrast. Most contemporary exegesis of the gospels of Matthew and Luke is built on the basis of such detailed observations.

In Matthew's version of Mark's narrative of the women at

the tomb (Matt. 28.1–10), the redactional changes are sufficiently significant to warrant giving the account in full:

> Now after the sabbath, towards the dawn of the first day of the week, Mary Magdalene and the other Mary went to see the sepulchre. And behold, there was a great earthquake; for an angel of the Lord descended from heaven and came and rolled back the stone, and sat upon it. His appearance was like lightning, and his raiment white as snow. And for fear of him the guards trembled and became like dead men. But the angel said to the women, 'Do not be afraid; for I know that you seek Jesus who was crucified. He is not here; for he has risen, as he said. Come, see the place where he lay. Then go quickly and tell his disciples that he has risen from the dead, and behold, he is going before you to Galilee; there you will see him. Lo, I have told you.' So they departed quickly from the tomb with fear and great joy, and ran to tell the disciples. And behold, Jesus met them and said, 'Hail!' And they came up and took hold of his feet and worshipped him. Then Jesus said to them, 'Do not be afraid; go and tell my brethren to go to Galilee, and there they will see me.'

There are three major redactional changes here from the Markan narrative: (1) the young man has become an angel, and details of the rolling away of the stone are given; (2) there is no reference to the women not fulfilling their responsibility – indeed, the supposition is that they did; and (3) the risen Jesus appears to the women. Then, in addition, there is the reference to the guards, but that is part of a Matthean apologetic legend that will concern us later. For the moment we will discuss the three major redactional changes.

(1) The angel and the rolling away of the stone

This need concern us only for a moment. For Matthew the resurrection of Jesus is a climax of God's redemptive activity on behalf of his people, and he and the tradition he represents have had a whole generation since Mark wrote to meditate on the event. So naturally the stories have begun to take on details more suitable to a supreme hierophany than the naturalistic young man and the simple discovery of the stone having been rolled away in Mark. These changes are simply testimony to the significance of the event for Matthew; they serve more to interpret the event than to provide additional narrative detail with regard to it.

(2) The women fulfilling their responsibility

There is in Matthew no trace of the theme of discipleship failure in connection with the women. Very much to the contrary, Matthew clearly implies that their natural fear on this occasion did not lead them to silence, as it does in Mark, but rather it was coupled with a great joy which overcame the fear and enabled them to fulfil their responsibility. This most important change must be seen as being due to two factors, one negative and one positive. Negatively, Matthew does not share the Markan view of discipleship failure, so he has no need to maintain the dark, enigmatic note on which the Gospel of Mark ends. Positively, he has a view of the resurrection very different from that of Mark; he has a view in which the resurrection is much more than a prelude to the parousia, it is the beginning of the whole new age of the church. So the women fulfil their responsibility, and provide the element of continuity which the Matthaean view of the resurrection of Jesus as the beginning of the age of the church demands. I shall discuss this particularly Matthaean view of the resurrection in detail later; for the moment I shall continue to follow Matthew's redaction of the Markan narrative.

(3) The appearance of the risen Lord to the women

This is a wholly new element in the narrative. Where Mark has no appearance stories at all, Matthew has two, of which the appearance to the women is the first. This story represents, therefore, the first element in the distinctively Matthaean understanding of the resurrection: the resurrection is of such a nature that the risen Lord can appear to the women, and commission them to an immediate task, for in this story the risen Lord repeats to the women the 'Go tell' instructions of the angel at the tomb. This indicates both an important aspect of Matthew's understanding of the resurrection – the risen Lord commissions people to a particular responsibility – and also the great significance he attaches to the appearance in Galilee, since in his narrative both the angel and the risen Lord emphasize it.

The new elements

In addition to the redaction of the Markan narrative, Matthew's resurrection narrative includes two wholly new elements: the story of the guard at the tomb, and the commissioning of the disciples in Galilee. The former is not of any great moment, but the latter is the climax of the whole gospel, as well as the key to Matthew's understanding of the resurrection.

(1) The story of the guard at the tomb

This story is in three parts. In Matthew 27.62–66 the Pharisees go to Pilate, remind him that Jesus said that after three days he would rise from the dead, and ask that a guard be set on the tomb so that Jesus' disciples might not be able to steal the body and pretend that Jesus rose from the dead. Pilate agrees to this, the tomb is sealed, and a guard is set. Then in 28.4, a redactional insertion into the empty tomb narrative, the guards see the angel and are terrified. Finally, in 28.11–15, the guards report what has happened to the chief priests and are bribed to tell the people that the disciples had stolen the body, 'and this story has been spread among the Jews to this day'.

One of the things we know about the Gospel of Matthew is that it was written in constant dialogue with a strong Jewish community; there is evidence of this in almost every chapter. Apparently this dialogue became rancorous, as is evident from Matthew's redactional additions to the 'woes' concerning wars against the Pharisees (Matt. 23.1–36; cf. Mark 12.37b–40), which in places are positively venomous. One rancorous element on the Jewish side must have been the claim that the disciples stole the body of Jesus, hid it, and then pretended that God had raised him from the dead, a calumny that has been repeated often enough since then. To meet this, Matthew, or the community he represented, developed this story about the guards at the tomb. It is obviously a legendary story because the situation it presupposes is historically impossible – the 'after three days' of the passion predictions comes from the evangelist Mark, and the idea of the resurrection of an individual as distinct from a general resurrection is a consequence of the Christian experience of Jesus as risen, not a presupposition of that experience. The story is an apologetic legend and need concern us no further. The validity of the claim 'Jesus is risen!' will not be determined for us by a legend designed to meet the calumny that his disciples had stolen his body.

(2) *The appearance to the disciples in Galilee*

Matthew 28.16–20 is often referred to as the 'great commission'. It reads as follows:

> Now the eleven disciples went to Galilee, to the mountain to which Jesus had directed them. And when they saw him they worshipped him; but some doubted. And Jesus came and said to them, 'All authority in heaven and on earth has been given to me. Go therefore and make disciples of all nations, baptizing them in the name of the Father and of the Son and of the Holy Spirit, teaching them to observe all that I have commanded you; and lo, I am with you always, to the close of the age.'

Matthew understands this appearance to the disciples in Galilee as fulfilling the promise of Jesus that they would 'see' him in Galilee, a promise Mark had understood would be fulfilled by the parousia. Also, where Mark had understood the reference to Galilee to be symbolic, Matthew understands it as literal and geographical. It is clearly very important indeed to Matthew, who not only reports the promise of Jesus from Mark 14.27 (Matt 26.32) and the repetition of it by the messenger at the tomb, but also has the risen Jesus repeat it to the women, as we have seen. Moreover, he emphasizes here in 28.16 that his appearance is the fulfilment of that promise, on 'the mountain to which Jesus had directed them'.

Although this is technically a resurrection appearance story, it is obvious that Matthew is comparatively uninterested in it as an appearance story, since he gives only the baldest possible details: 'When they saw him they worshipped him; but some doubted.' When one compares this to the parallel story in Luke 24.36–49, and notes the details given there, then this appears bald indeed. Matthew's whole interest lies in the words of Jesus, the act of commissioning the disciples; for the rest he gives only sufficient detail to set the stage for that commissioning. It is for this reason that scholars tend to refer to this narrative as 'the great commission' or something similar, rather than as 'the appearance to the disciples in Galilee'.

The act of commissioning the disciples takes the form of a five-part statement by Jesus, every part of which demands the most careful consideration. I will therefore examine each part in turn.

'All authority in heaven and on earth has been given to me.' In Matthew's understanding, Jesus appears to his disciples not only as risen from the dead but also as having been granted 'all authority in heaven and on earth'. From the moment of his resurrection he already possesses the power which he will exercise on earth prior to and in anticipation of his parousia. This is an important step in the development of a theology of the resurrection. Whereas Mark understood Jesus to have been taken by God to be with Moses and Elijah in the heavens, whence he would come to exercise his power and authority as Son of man *at his parousia,* Matthew understands the risen Jesus as already exercising aspects of that power and authority *through the church*. I will justify the 'through the church' immediately below.

'Go therefore and make disciples of all nations.' This is the world-wide mission of the church, as Matthew understands it. As Jesus 'made disciples', so the church is to go out into all the world and 'make disciples'. We may use the

word *church* in this connection because Matthew has earlier used it; indeed, he is the only gospel writer who does so. In 16.18 we find the famous 'You are Peter, and upon this rock I will build my church', and in 18.17 as part of a major discourse to the disciples, not to a crowd, we read, 'If he refuses to listen to them [two or three witnesses], tell it to the church; and if he refuses to listen even to the church, let him be to you as a Gentile and a tax collector.' Clearly Matthew thinks of the group of Jesus' disciples as already the embryonic church, and certainly he thinks of the group of further disciples whom those disciples will 'make' as the church.

'Baptizing them in the name of the Father and of the Son and of the Holy Spirit.' This is remarkable for its clear use of the trinitarian formula developed in the early church; it is one of the most ecclesiastical statements in the New Testament. It is also ecclesiastical in the sense that it envisages baptism as an initiation rite by means of which the Christian community separates itself and its members from any other community, especially in this instance the Jewish community. Christians now have a physical means of defining themselves as a community, a symbolic act which gives them identity as a community.

'Teaching them to observe all that I have commanded you.' This is in many ways the most remarkable and the most important of all the parts of this commissioning, for it expresses exactly what it means for Matthew to be a believer in a world in which Jesus is risen. Let me begin our discussion of it with a redaction-critical observation: this is the first time in the whole gospel in which Matthew uses the verb *to teach* in connection with the disciples. He frequently uses it of Jesus (e.g. 4.23; 5.2, the beginning of the Sermon on the Mount; 9.35; 11.1; 13.54). He follows Mark where Mark uses it of Jesus (e.g. 7.29 || Mark 1.22; 13.54 || Mark 6.2). He even adds it in places where Mark does not have it (e.g. 21.23 || Mark 11.28; 22.16 || Mark 12.14). But he never uses it of the disciples until the commissioning scene, and he carefully avoids it in places where Mark uses it of the

disciples (e.g. Mark 6.30 || Matt. 14.13). The one possible exception to this rule is Matthew 5.19, but as we shall see below, this is in fact the exception that proves the rule.

I turn next to two literary-critical observations, observations based on a careful study of the way in which Matthew has composed his gospel as a whole. The first such observation is that there is in the Gospel of Matthew a hinge chapter, a chapter in the course of which the tenor of the whole changes dramatically. This is chapter 13, the parable chapter. Up to that point Matthew depicts Jesus as addressing himself to the Jewish people as a whole – to, as it were, the 'old' Israel of God. But in chapters 11 and 12 he emphasizes a growing tension between Jesus and 'the crowds', 'the cities', 'the Pharisees', 'the people', and 'the scribes and the Pharisees', while at the same time he portrays Jesus as making strong christological claims (e.g. 11.25–30; 12.30–32). Then in 12.44–50, he offers a version of Mark 3.31–35, an incident concerning who the true relatives of Jesus may be said to be, in which he adds a redactional element: 'And stretching out his hand towards his disciples, he said, "Here are my mother and my brothers!" ' The reference to the disciples is a redactional insertion by Matthew into the Markan narrative, and it points forward to what is to come in his own narrative.

Chapter 13 is the hinge chapter, and the hinge comes at verse 36, where Jesus left 'the crowds' and his disciples 'came to him'. Up to that point Matthew has in general in this chapter been following his source, Mark 4, the parable chapter in Mark, except that he has introduced a new parable, the parable of the weeds (Matt. 13.24–30). But now he goes his own way and, in particular, he introduces an interpretation of this parable which makes it an allegory of the Christian church (13.36–43). He introduces a further parable, the parable of the net, which is itself a further allegory of the church (13.47–50), and he concludes the discourse with the saying, 'Every scribe who has been trained for the kingdom of heaven is like a householder who brings out of his treasure what is new and what is old.'

Then Matthew offers his version of Jesus' rejection in 'his own country' (Matt. 13.53–58 || Mark 6.1–6) and from that point forward his narrative depicts Jesus as being concerned almost exclusively with his disciples, the 'new' Israel of God, as it were, until we reach Jerusalem and the final rejection of Jesus by the 'old' Israel of God.

Thus Matthew deliberately thematizes his narrative. Down to 13.36 Jesus addresses himself to the Jewish people, and finds them increasingly hostile. After 13.36 Jesus addresses himself to his disciples, except in the case of two hostile intrusions by representatives of the Jewish people (16.1–4; 19.3–9). Then in 13.53–58 we have the rejection of Jesus 'in his own country', which anticipates the final rejection of Jesus by his own people in Jerusalem. So there is a dramatic shift in the narrative of the Gospel of Matthew at 13.36, a shift from Jesus and the old Israel of God to Jesus and the new Israel of God.

The second literary-critical observation is that Matthew stylizes the major elements of the teaching of Jesus into five great discourses, to each one of which he calls special attention by ending it with a formula such as 'when Jesus finished these sayings'. These discourses are found as follows:

	Discourse	*Formula*
5.1–7.2	The Sermon on the Mount	7.28
10.5–42	The Missionary Discourse	11.1
13.1–52	The Parable (and Hinge) Chapter	13.53
18.1–35	Christian Community Regulations	19.1
24.3–25.46	Apocalyptic Discourse	26.1

It is interesting to note that the subjects of the discourses bear out the shift of concern at 13.36. The two discourses which follow that hinge chapter are concerned with Christian community regulations and with the future of the Christian community in the world – the latter because Matthew's apocalyptic discourse has a whole series of parables in chapter 25 which are all allegories of the prospects of the Christian church at the parousia. But more important for our immediate purpose is the fact that there are five of these discourses, the first of which is on a mountain. This has to be an echo of the fact that the Torah, the law of Moses, was in five books, and that it was traditionally revealed to Moses on Mount Sinai. Matthew is claiming that the teaching of Jesus is the new Torah, the new verbal revelation of God to his people, and that as such it supersedes the law of Moses.

Now we can see why the disciples never 'teach' in the Gospel of Matthew, and why there is such an emphasis upon Jesus 'teaching'. The disciples never teach because the teaching is the new verbal revelation which only Jesus can give, and the fact of Jesus teaching is constantly emphasized because this teaching is the new verbal revelation and as such the most important aspect of Jesus' earthly activity.

This brings me to the one apparent exception to this: 'Whoever then relaxes one of the least of these commandments and teaches men so, shall be called least in the kingdom of heaven; but he who does them and teaches them shall be called great in the kingdom of heaven' (Matt. 5.19). This certainly implies that the disciples who are part of the audience of the Sermon on the Mount, from which this saying is taken, are to teach. But notice what it is that they are to teach – 'the commandments' – and that they are not to 'relax' the commandments. In other words, they are to teach the tenets of the verbal revelation of God, and they are to interpret those tenets in the proper manner. That the concern here is the *new* verbal revelation of God is evident, both from the fact that this saying is from the first 'book' of that new verbal revelation, and from its verbal similarity to the statement of Jesus to his disciples at the point in the Gospel of Matthew where he has turned to them exclusively – a statement wherein he describes a disciple as a 'scribe who has been trained for the kingdom of heaven' (Matt. 13.52). It is evident that Matthew regards a disciple as 'teaching' when he transmits and interprets, as a 'scribe who has been trained for the kingdom of heaven', the tenets of the new verbal revelation of God to his people, the teaching of Jesus.

I have gone through this long and complex argument to justify a particular interpretation of the aspect of the commissioning of the disciples which concerns 'teaching them to observe all that I have commanded you'. In view of the exegesis and arguments I have given above I may now claim that this is a commission to teach and to interpret authoritatively the new verbal revelation of God to his people, the tenets of the teaching of Jesus.

With this we have reached the heart of Matthew's understanding of what it means to live in a world in which Jesus is risen. It means to accept the privileges and responsibilities of a life lived in response to the new verbal revelation of God to his people through Jesus Christ, as this revelation is authoritatively interpreted by the church specifically commissioned to this task by the risen Jesus himself.

'And lo, I am with you always, to the close of the age.' I am developing the thesis that whereas Mark sees the resurrection of Jesus only as a necessary prelude to his parousia, Matthew sees it as the occasion for the commissioning of the disciples as the Christian church, and hence as the inauguration of a distinctive new age, the age of the Christian church. But there is a definite limit set to this age, the limit of 'the close of the age', the limit of the parousia. In this final element of the commissioning Matthew sets this limit, the limit of 'the close of the age', as he has already done in his interpretation of the parable of the weeds (13.39–49), and also in his introduction to the apocalyptic discourse (24.3). This last reference is particularly interesting in that it equates 'the close of the age' with the parousia. *Parousia* is a technical term in the New Testament for the coming of Jesus as Son of man, and Matthew uses it in this way in 24:3: 'What will be the sign of your coming [Greek: *parousia*] and of the close of the age?' This is the introduction to the apocalyptic discourse, and Matthew continues to use the term in this way throughout the discourse (24.27, 37, 39). So we can see that Matthew is concerned to make

and to maintain the point that the age inaugurated by the resurrection of Jesus, the age within which the church is commissioned to work, is an age to which a definite limit will be set by 'the close of the age', by the parousia of Jesus.

The second important aspect of this last element in the commissioning address is the promise of the risen Lord to his church, 'I am with you always . . . ' This is a theme which Matthew had sounded earlier in his gospel. The most notable instances are in the stilling of the storm (Matt. 8.23–27 || Mark 4.36–41), where Matthew's redactional changes – the insertion of the liturgical 'Save us, Lord; we are perishing', the insertion of the ecclesiastical 'men of little faith', the change of the place of the dialogue from after the miracle to before it – transform a Markan miracle story into an allegory of the church; and in part of the discourse on Christian community regulations (18:20): 'Where two or three are gathered in my name, there am I in the midst of them.' Matthew is concerned to stress the fact that as the church sets out to fulfil the responsibility for which she is commissioned, the risen Lord is present in her midst.

Summary

I am now in a position to make a brief, summary statement about the resurrection narratives in the Gospel of Matthew. Matthew sees the resurrection of Jesus as inaugurating a new age in the history of mankind and of mankind's relationship with God. It inaugurates the age of the church, an age to be brought to an end by the parousia. So Jesus appears to the women, the women fulfil their responsibility, and the necessary continuity between the fate of Jesus and the life of the Christian church is established. The disciples then gather in Galilee and the risen Lord appears to them to commission them as the nucleus of the Christian church in the world, and to alert them to the specific responsibilities and privileges of that church in the world.

A particularly significant aspect of the commissioning scene is the way in which the whole emphasis is upon the address by Jesus, and the way in which this address summarizes major tenets of the Matthaean theology. Matthew sees God in his relationship to mankind through Jesus, and specifically in the verbal revelation of the teaching of Jesus. Then he sees mankind in its relationship to God as in a relationship determined by mankind's obedience to the verbal revelation, as that revelation is authoritatively interpreted by the church. Further, the church is guided in her task, and the believer sustained in his or hers, by the continuing presence of the risen Lord in his church. These themes all come to expression in the commissioning scene, and in retrospect they can be seen as themes that have dominated the Gospel of Matthew as a whole.

The Matthaean resurrection narratives as myth

The effect of the resurrection narratives in the Gospel of Matthew is to make the story of Jesus the foundation myth of Christian origins. Matthew was writing for a generation of Christians which had an urgent need, the need to identify themselves as *Christians* and to satisfy themselves that they had a place both in the world and in the purpose of God. The generation for which Mark wrote was still fundamentally *Jewish;* it identified itself out of the great myth of Jewish origins, the narrative of Moses, David, and the prophets. Mark's generation lived out of the Jewish apocalyptic hope for the imminent appearance of the apocalyptic hero as judge and redeemer, as did Mark himself. True, it identified this hero as the Son of man, Jesus of Nazareth, and therein lay the seeds of ultimate disruption between itself and the Jewish communities. However, the structures of faith and practice were still fundamentally Jewish, and the foundation myth was still the Jewish foundation myth. But by the time of Matthew, one generation later, all this had changed, and that for two reasons.

In the first place Jerusalem had fallen; the Temple had been destroyed; the inviolable had been violated. It is impossible for us to reconstruct today the enormous impact of the fall of Jerusalem and the destruction of its temple upon both Jewish and incipient Christian communities. It literally changed everything for them. Both survived only by finding a whole new way of identifying themselves, and of assuring themselves that this was still God's world and that they had a place in it. The Jewish communities did this through the Pharisees, a group of whom settled in a place called Jamnia and there established Judaism as the religion of verbal revelation – the Torah – and of obedience to that revelation as authoritatively established by the rabbi. The Temple was not needed any more. The navel of the universe was no longer the hill, Mount Zion, in Jerusalem; it was the word of God, the Torah, and this could be read and interpreted anywhere and everywhere.

The Jewish response to the fall of Jerusalem was both magnificent and successful. What the Pharisees at Jamnia established was essentially the rabbinic Judaism which survived into the modern world, and which still survives. The incipient Christians, however, took a different path. For them the navel of the universe became the story of Jesus, who in himself became the new temple and the new Mount Zion. In the case of the evangelist Matthew, the story of Jesus became the means of the new and decisive revelation of God to man, and obedience to that revelation became the key to life in the world. There are striking phenomenological parallels between Matthew and the Pharisees at Jamnia. Both understood religion as essentially a matter of response to verbal revelation, and both felt the need for the revelation to be authoritatively interpreted within the community of which it was the constitutive base. But Matthew saw Jesus as the organ of a verbal revelation which superseded the Torah of Moses, and therein lay the need for a foundation myth of *Christian* origins, which his gospel provides.

The interpretation of the Matthaean resurrection narratives

Again, I claim here no authority as a New Testament scholar, but write only out of personal conviction, although I hope the conviction is informed by the scholarship. In a sense Matthew is easier to interpret than is Mark, because in Matthew the primordial myth has become foundation myth, and the primordial theme is muted by the concern for the church and the life of the believer in the church. Moreover, the parousia is no longer the central focus of concern. Although the parousia is expected, it is no longer regarded as imminent, and the central focus of concern has become the church in the world 'to the close of the age'. We no longer have to wrestle with primordial themes and the parousia, but can begin with the church.

The Gospel of Matthew has always been regarded as 'the church's book', and when the New Testament was collected as a unit this gospel was put first. One can see why that should be. In the Matthaean version of the confession of Peter at Caesarea Philippi (16.13–23) we have the long insertion in which Jesus says to Peter, 'And I tell you, you are Peter, and on this rock I will build my church, and the powers of death shall not prevail against it'; also, the main concern in the resurrection narratives is the commissioning of the disciples to form the church. Moreover, the last element of that commission is the promise, 'Lo, I am with you always, to the close of the age.'

The famous German New Testament scholar and theologian Rudolf Bultmann is well known for his claim that to say 'Jesus is risen!' is to say that Jesus is risen into the kerygma, into the proclamation of the church. I would like to plagiarize Bultmann and say that to speak of the resurrection in Matthaean terms is to say that Jesus makes possible the life of the church, and the life of the church is the validation of the claim, 'Jesus is risen!' It is in the church that one finds the presence of the risen Lord; it is the presence of the risen Lord within the church that transforms the life of the believer. As for the parousia, to say 'to the close of the age' is to say that ultimately all things – the world, the church, and the believer – are in the hands of God.

4

THE RESURRECTION NARRATIVES IN THE GOSPEL OF LUKE

Luke's redaction of the Markan narrative

As in the chapter dealing with the Gospel of Matthew, I will begin this chapter on Luke with a discussion of the redaction of the Markan narrative. Luke 23.49–56 follows the general theme of the Markan narrative of the women at the cross and the burial. But it abbreviates the Markan narrative by not naming the women, while expanding it with careful explanation of particular Jewish customs – for example: 'On the sabbath day they rested according to the commandment.' Luke 24.1–11 is the Lukan version of the narrative of the women at the tomb, and I give it here in full.

> But on the first day of the week, at early dawn, they went to the tomb, taking the spices which they had prepared. And they found the stone rolled away from the tomb, but when they went in they did not find the body. While they were perplexed about this, behold, two men stood by them in dazzling apparel; and as they were frightened and bowed their faces to the ground, the men said to them, 'Why do you seek the living among the dead? Remember how he told you while he was still in Galilee, that the Son of man must be delivered into the hands of sinful men, and be crucified, and on the third day rise.' And they remembered his words, and returning from the tomb they told all this to the eleven and to all the rest. Now it was Mary Magdalene and Joanna and Mary the mother of James and the other women with them who told this to the apostles; but these words seemed to them an idle tale, and they did not believe them.

The first and most obvious thing about this narrative is that it is much smoother and better-told than Mark's, but then Luke is the most consummate literary artist in the New Testament. The second redactional element is that the young man of the Markan narrative has become 'two men in dazzling apparel'. This is more restrained than the parallel Matthaean redaction, but it serves the same general purpose. Luke too represents a tradition that had meditated on this world-shattering event for a generation longer than had Mark. But the most interesting redactional element in this narrative is the third, namely, the fact that the message to the women no longer concerns seeing Jesus in Galilee, but is a passion prediction like the one in Mark 9.31.

This is a most dramatic change, and it leads us to check the Lukan versions of the Markan passion predictions and of the promise of Jesus, 'I will go before you to Galilee', in Mark 14.28. If we do this we find that Luke has reasonable facsimiles of the passion predictions (Mark 8.31 || Luke 9.22; Mark 9.31 || Luke 9.44; Mark 10.33–34 || Luke 18.32–33) except that the second is abbreviated to 'the Son of man is to be delivered into the hands of men'. But the promise of Jesus to his disciples has completely disappeared from the Lukan narrative; Mark 14.27–28 has no equivalent at all in Luke. It would have to come after Luke 22.39, and it is simply not there. What has happened is that Luke has simply obliterated all reference to the disciples seeing Jesus in Galilee after his death, and he has filled the gap left by this in the message to the women at the tomb by using a passion prediction. This is a bold step and, as we shall see, Luke has very strong theological reasons for taking it.

A fourth redactional change in this narrative as compared to its Markan source is that Luke specifically stated that the women fulfilled their trust and 'told all this to the eleven and to all the rest'. As was Matthew, Luke is very much concerned with the element of continuity between the fate of Jesus and the origins of the Christian church, and he also has an interest in the Markan theme of total discipleship failure. Unlike Matthew, however, he has no account of a resurrection appearance to the women.

The new elements

There are three new elements in the Lukan narrative as compared to the Markan: an appearance of the risen Jesus to two disciples on the Emmaus road; an appearance to the disciples as a group in Jerusalem; and the ascension of Jesus into heaven. We will discuss each of these in turn.

(1) The Emmaus road narrative (Luke 24.13–35)

This is one of the best known and most loved of the gospel stories; it represents the consummate literary art of the evangelist Luke at his best. Two disciples of Jesus are walking the seven miles or so from Jerusalem to Emmaus, discussing with one another 'all these things that had happened'. The risen Jesus meets them and joins with them, but they do not recognize him. But they fall into conversation with him, and they discuss with him 'the things that had happened' in Jerusalem 'in these days', namely, the things concerning the life and fate of Jesus of Nazareth, and rumours concerning his resurrection. Jesus then interprets the whole matter from the scriptures: 'Beginning with Moses and all the prophets, he interpreted to them in all the scriptures the things concerning himself' (24.27). Still the disciples do not recognize him, but they persuade him to spend the night with them, and then, at the evening meal, 'when he was at table with them, he took the bread and blessed, and broke it, and gave it to them. And their eyes were opened and they recognized him; and he vanished out of their sight.' The two return to Jerusalem where they find the other disciples gathered together, and they are told, 'The Lord has risen indeed, and has appeared to Simon!' They then tell the others of their experience on the Emmaus road.

There are aspects of this narrative which require detailed discussion, the first of which is the reported appearance to Simon (Peter).

The reported appearance to Simon (Peter). A first thing to be noted about the Emmaus road narrative is that it reports, at second hand, this appearance. The early tradition of resurrection appearances reported by Paul (I Cor. 15.5–7) also begins with a reference to an appearance to Peter. (Paul calls him Cephas, which is the Aramaic equivalent of Peter – they probably always talked together in Aramaic, so Paul thinks of the name in Aramaic.) No tradition of this appearance has survived in the New Testament unless, as has been suggested, the Matthaean redactional insertion into the Markan account of the confession at Caesarea Philippi (Matt. 16.17–19), with its commissioning of Peter as head of the church, is a remnant of such a tradition. That is an interesting suggestion, but the fact remains that no formal account of an appearance to Peter has survived in the gospels.

A second thing to be noted about this narrative is the strong emphasis upon the necessity of interpreting and understanding the life and fate of Jesus through the scriptures.

Interpreting the life and fate of Jesus through the scriptures. This is a major emphasis of the evangelist Luke, as can be seen perhaps best from Luke 4.16–20, the rejection at Nazareth. In Luke's source, the Gospel of Mark, it is a transitional unit (6.1–6) bringing to an end the first major section of the gospel (1.21–5.43). In this section Jesus is depicted as mighty in deed and word, and Mark ends the section with the theme of rejection, a theme that is to grow in importance until we reach the cross, where Jesus is rejected by his people, the Jews, and by his disciples, and even abandoned by God. This is all part of the great primordial theme of suffering/death/overcoming of death which dominates the Gospel of Mark, and which I discussed above. The progressively total rejection of Jesus is a major element in the suffering motif. Luke completely changes the function of the rejection pericope (Mark 6.1–6). First of all he transposes it to the very beginning of the first phase of the ministry of Jesus, rather than at its end. Then he transforms the pericope by introducing a wholly new element:

> And he stood up to read; and there was given to him the book of the prophet Isaiah. He opened the book and found the place where it was written, 'The Spirit of the Lord is upon me, because he has anointed me to preach good news to the poor. He has sent me to proclaim release to the captives and recovering of sight to the blind, to set at liberty those who are oppressed, to proclaim the acceptable year of the Lord.' And he closed the book, and gave it back to the attendant, and sat down; and the eyes of all in the synagogue were fixed on him. And he began to say to them, 'Today this scripture has been fulfilled in your hearing' (Luke 4.16b–21).

The effect of this redactional insertion, and of the further redactional changes which Luke introduces into his Markan source (cf. Luke 4.16–30 and Mark 6.1–6), is to change the whole tenor of the pericope. Now it becomes a frontispiece, introducing and interpreting the whole ministry of Jesus as Luke understands it. Luke pursues the theme of the Isaiah quotation throughout his presentation of that ministry. But my concern at the moment is to point out that Luke's whole interpretation of the ministry of Jesus is dependent upon a quotation of scripture; the whole ministry is seen as a fulfilment of scripture.

This is perhaps the most spectacular instance of Luke's concern for the fulfilment of scripture, but it is by no means isolated. Luke pursues the theme of scriptural fulfilment throughout his gospel, and indeed through the Acts of the Apostles, so that the emphasis upon it in the Emmaus road story – 'And beginning with Moses and all the prophets, he interpreted to them in all the scriptures the things concerning himself' (24.27) – is a reiteration of a major Lukan theme.

The risen Christ's interpretation of the scriptures. A third element to be noted in this narrative is the risen Christ's particular interpretation of the scriptures. In the Emmaus road narrative the risen Christ draws a particular lesson from the scriptures as he interprets them for these two disciples: 'Was it not necessary that the Christ should suffer these things and enter into his glory?' (24.26). The interesting thing here is that the suffering has become a means of entering into glory: the passion has become an apotheosis. When one compares Luke's account of the crucifixion (Luke 23.33–49) with his Markan source (Mark 15.33–47) one can see how much he has transformed it in the interests of this understanding of the passion. The derision of Jesus in Mark 15.29–30 has been reduced to 'If you are the King of the Jews, save yourself!' (Luke 23.37). The brief mention in Mark 15.32 that 'those who were with him also reviled him' has been expanded into a passage in which one of the criminals rebukes his companion, asking, 'Jesus, remember me when you come into your kingdom', and is promised by Jesus, 'Today you will be with me in Paradise' (Luke 23.39–43). The cry of dereliction (Mark 15.34) is gone, and in its place we have the sovereign, 'Father, into thy hands I commit my spirit!' (Luke 23.46). The cumulative effect of these and other, smaller redactional changes is remarkable: they make the crucifixion a means whereby the Christ enters 'into his glory'. So, again, the Emmaus road narrative summarizes a major theme of the gospel as a whole.

The emphasis upon the eucharist. A last thing to be noted about the Emmaus road narrative is that there is a strong emphasis upon the eucharist in it. The two disciples recognize Jesus as 'he took the bread and blessed, and broke it, and gave it to them' (Luke 24.30). Further, when they return to Jerusalem the disciples tell 'how he was known to them in the breaking of the bread' (24.35). This is undoubtedly a reference to the eucharist. Luke is telling his readers that the risen Lord can be known to them, as he became known to these two disciples, in the eucharist. The evangelist is concerned to build a bridge between Jesus as he was in his ministry – and as he can be known as risen – and the believer who reads his two-volume Luke–Acts. So he constantly represents Jesus at prayer, attending the synagogue 'as his custom was' (4.16), being led and guided by the Spirit of God, and so on – all things which in their turn the apostles do and experience in Acts, and all things which the believer in his or her turn can do in the Christian community. So here in the Emmaus road story we have a particular example of this bridge-building between Jesus and Luke's reader; the reader can know Jesus as risen in the eucharist.

(2) The appearance to the disciples as a group in Jerusalem (Luke 24.36–49)

This narrative breaks naturally into two parts, 24.36–43 and 24.44–49. The first part is essentially an apologetic legend; the second is a speech by the risen Jesus.

The apologetic legend (Luke 24.36–43). In this part of the narrative Jesus appears to the disciples as a group, 'but they were startled and frightened, and supposed that they saw a spirit'. But Jesus asks them to look at his hands and feet, to handle him – 'for a spirit has not flesh and bones as you see that I have' – and asks for, takes, and eats 'a piece of broiled fish'. This part of the narrative is an apologetic legend, like the story of the guard at the tomb in Matthew, except that it is directed to a different goal. In Matthew the problem was the Jewish calumny that the disciples had stolen the body of Jesus in order to pretend that he was risen from the dead. In Luke the problem was that in the Hellenistic Greek world it was widely assumed that a religious hero overcame death by being transformed into a spiritual being who no longer had any contact with the essentially unreal world of flesh, blood, and bodies. The Hellenistic Greek world would readily have acclaimed the resurrection of Jesus as an escape from the world of flesh, blood, and bodies into the world of disembodied spirit, and Jesus would thereby have joined a pantheon of religious heroes in which there was always room for one more. But the evangelist Luke, or the community from which he writes, resisted this tendency to assimilate Jesus into a pantheon of Hellenistic Greek religious heroes by developing an apologetic legend of the corporeality of Jesus as risen. Jesus as risen is not a disembodied spiritual being: he can be seen, touched and handled; he eats a piece of broiled fish. As in the case of the Matthaean apologetic legend, this is also not a narrative that is addressed to a question that is real to us. Our acceptance or rejection of the claim 'Jesus is risen!' will not be determined by a legend concerning the corporeality of his presence as he appeared to his disciples.

The speech of the risen Jesus (Luke 24.44–49). In the second part of this narrative the risen Jesus makes a speech which is, in effect, a major statement of the Lukan theology. It begins with the restatement of a theme prominent in the Emmaus road story, the need to interpret the Christ event in the light of the scriptures: ' "These are my words which I spoke to you while I was still with you, that everything about me in the law of Moses and the prophets and the psalms must be fulfilled." Then he opened their minds to understand the scriptures.' The statement then continues with what is, in effect, a summary of a major aspect of what the evangelist and the church for which he writes have learned from the scripture: 'Thus it is written that the Christ should suffer and on the third day rise from the dead.' This is a passion prediction, and as such it echoes the message to the women at the tomb, which I discussed above. Notice that it is a variant of, and in the mind of Luke obviously equivalent to, the theme sounded in the Emmaus road story: 'Was it not necessary that the Christ should suffer these things and enter into his glory?' For Luke to say that the Christ should 'rise from the dead' is to say that he should 'enter his glory'. This is an important insight into Luke's understanding of the resurrection, and it will concern us further below.

The speech of the risen Jesus then continues with a statement of the Lukan understanding of the foundation myth of Christian origins, 'that repentance and forgiveness of sins should be preached in his name to all nations, beginning from Jerusalem'. The evangelist Luke has an understanding of the Christian church, and of the situation of the Christian believer in the world, every bit as distinctive as that of the evangelist Matthew, and quite different from it. Like Matthew he faces the problem of finding a means of self-identity for the fledgling Christian community which could no longer identify itself in terms of the Jewish foundation myth. But one suspects that in his case the need was created not so much by hostility and rejection on the part of a specific Jewish community as it was by simple loss of contact with Hellenistic Judaism and the increasing threat of absorption into the vast and multitudinous world of Hellenistic religiosity. But whatever the particular historical and cultural reasons might be, clearly the community or communities out of which and for which Luke wrote were desperately in need of a distinctively Christian foundation myth. I am not claiming that the evangelist recognized this need and self-consciously set out to meet it; what I am claiming is that this need has shaped his understanding of the story of Jesus and the apostles, whether consciously or unconsciously.

We saw earlier that for Matthew the heart of the matter was the new verbal revelation of God in the teaching of Jesus and its authoritative interpretation by the church. For Luke, on the other hand, the heart of the matter lies in the idea of a sacred centre, a *place* where God is particularly to be found and known. Luke is heir to a tradition in which Jerusalem was what one might call 'the navel of the universe', the place above all others where God was to be found and known, the place above all places sacred and inviolable as the holiest of all holy places. Both Hellenistic Judaism and the Hellenistic Jewish Christianity which Luke ultimately represents lived out of the conviction that whatever might be true of Antioch or Corinth or Rome, Jerusalem was holy; in Jerusalem God was particularly and peculiarly to be found and known.

But Jerusalem fell to the Romans in the Jewish War of AD 66–70. Roman soldiers tramped through the Temple of God at their pleasure; the Holy of Holies became simply a dusty room to be used for any purpose a Roman soldier might see fit. The inviolable was violated. The event of the fall of

Jerusalem and the destruction of its temple in AD 70 sent a shock wave through Hellenistic Judaism and Hellenistic Jewish Christianity, the force of which it would be difficult to exaggerate. Indeed Hellenistic Judaism itself perished in the convulsions which followed. But Hellenistic Jewish Christianity survived. It survived because it found a new sacred centre in the Christian movement itself: the life of Jesus became the navel of the universe, the place where God was particularly to be found and known.

Luke pursues this theme throughout his two-volume work. He presents the life of Jesus as a sacred time, a time of fulfilment, blessing and revelation. He presents Jerusalem as the place where Jesus is rejected and the place, therefore, that God himself rejects. But Jerusalem is the place where God himself makes a new beginning, for the rejection of Jesus ends in the triumph of God, the passion culminates in the resurrection, and the risen Jesus appears to his disciples *in Jerusalem*. The Christian movement starts in Jerusalem, and in the Acts of the Apostles, Luke portrays its inevitable progress to the symbolic centre of the world, to Rome. It is the Christian movement itself which in its inevitable progress from Jerusalem to Rome becomes the new sacred centre; the members of this movement relate to the sacred time of Jesus, and wherever the gospel of repentance and the forgiveness of sins is preached, *there* is 'the navel of the universe'.

This Lukan theological construction is breathtaking in its boldness of conception. It was also effective. The believer could see in the time of Jesus the sacred time of fulfilment and revelation; the believer could find in the Christian movement the means of relating to that sacred person and that sacred time as he or she responded to the preaching of the gospel. Moreover the believer was bound to Jesus by one further factor: the believer was empowered by that same spirit which had empowered Jesus himself. This is the import of the last element in this speech of the risen Lord to his disciples: 'You are witnesses of these things. And behold, I send the promise of my Father upon you; but stay in the city, until you are clothed with power from on high' (Luke 24.48–49).

In the Gospel of Luke there is an enormous emphasis upon the Spirit of God, the Holy Spirit. This can be seen in the Lukan account of the baptism of Jesus (3.21–22), when it is compared with its source (Mark 1.9–11). The Markan account narrates a baptism: 'Jesus . . . was baptized by John in the Jordan', and an accompanying descent of the Spirit: 'and when he came up out of the water, immediately he saw the heavens opened and the Spirit descending upon him like a dove'. But in Luke all this is changed, and we read, 'Now when all the people were baptized, and when Jesus also had been baptized and was praying, the heaven was opened, and the Holy Spirit descended upon him in bodily form as a dove.' The baptism has been relegated to one of three antecedent clauses – all the people baptized, Jesus baptized, Jesus praying – which serve to set the stage for the action of the main verbs – the heavens are opened, the Spirit descends. If we did not read Luke in the light of Mark we would not call this pericope 'the baptism of Jesus'; we would call it 'the descent of the Spirit upon Jesus'. This emphasis upon the Spirit continues throughout the Gospel of Luke. I called attention above to the synagogue scene at Nazareth (Luke 4.16–20), the frontispiece of the account of the ministry of Jesus, where part of the prophecy that is fulfilled is, 'The Spirit of the Lord is upon me', and to the Lukan account of the crucifixion, wherein Jesus formally returns the Spirit to the Father.

The same emphasis is found in the Acts of the Apostles. The descent of the Spirit upon the apostles at Pentecost (Acts 2.1–13) is interpreted as a baptism in Acts 1.5: 'before many days you shall be baptized with the Holy Spirit'. As the gospel begins with a baptism/descent of the Spirit, so also does the Acts of the Apostles, and the parallelism continues with references to the work of the Spirit, as frequent and as important in Acts as they are in the gospel. Clearly Luke sees Jesus and the apostles as inspired by the same Spirit.

(3) *The Ascension (Luke 24.50–53)*

> Then he led them out as far as Bethany, and lifting up his hands he blessed them. While he blessed them he parted from them and was carried up into heaven. And they returned to Jerusalem with great joy, and were continually in the temple praising God.

The reference to the ascension in these verses is not textually certain; some ancient manuscripts omit 'and was carried up into heaven'. The difficulty of the question can be seen from the fact that the first edition of the Revised Standard Version (1952) relegated the reference to the margin, while the second (1971) restored it to the text. It should, however, be read in the text. Not only is it the natural climax of the gospel itself, but also its omission is readily explicable by the fact that in the ancient uncial manuscripts the letters before and after it read *NKAI*. Some ancient scribe's eye inadvertently looked down from the one and up to the other, a mistake frequently found, and the manuscript he copied became the ancestor of the 'some ancient manuscripts' which omit the reference.

So far as we can tell, the evangelist Luke is the first Christian writer to understand the ascension as an event distinct from the resurrection itself. As we have seen, Mark understands Jesus as being raised by God directly into the heavens; and in Matthew, when Jesus appears to the disciples as a group in Galilee he already possesses his full and ultimate authority – it is an appearance from the heavens. It seems probable that the first appearance stories were not stories of the risen Jesus appearing to his disciples, the women, and so on, before being taken up into heaven, but appearances of the risen Lord *from* heaven, appearances proleptic of the parousia. By the nature of things we can never be sure of this – but certainly not in I Corinthians 15.3–8, nor in Mark, nor in Matthew, is there any hint of an ascension as separate from a resurrection. In Luke–Acts, however, all this changes, and the ascension becomes a separate event.

This change is a consequence of a change in the understanding of the nature of the relationship between Jesus and his disciples. First, there is the earthly ministry of Jesus with his disciples, culminating in the cross. Then follows the resurrection and an interim period of teaching of the disciples by the risen Jesus, culminating in the ascension. Finally, the disciples become the apostles of the early church. As a matter of fact, one can see the seeds of future development in the differences between the Gospel of Luke and the Acts of the Apostles in this regard. In the gospel, with his attention fixed on the ministry of Jesus, the appearance stories are appearance stories, the teaching of the risen Jesus to his disciples is brief, and the reference to the ascension is minimal. But in Acts 1.3–11 the 'appearance story' is really 'the further ministry of Jesus, as Jesus risen from the dead, with his disciples', and the description of the ascension is much more elaborate. But now the attention of the author is upon the early church and upon the necessity of fulfilling the instructions of the risen Lord to its first leaders.

Summary

It is clear that as we move from Mark to Matthew to Luke there are very real changes and developments in the understanding of the resurrection. If we take the matter of appearance stories, Mark has none; Matthew has one to the women – a very brief one probably intended to fill what was for Matthew an obvious lacuna in the text of Mark – and one to the disciples as a group, a story in which Jesus appears in his heavenly authority, apparently from the heavens. Then Luke has appearances to the two disciples on the Emmaus road, and to the disciples as a group. But these are followed by the ascension, and the Jesus who appears is still a very human Jesus. These appearances continue the ministry of Jesus with his disciples between the resurrection and the ascension.

I noted earlier that Luke understands the resurrection of

Jesus as Jesus 'entering into his glory'. This is shown by the juxtaposition of predictions of the passion and resurrection at the empty tomb, and in the appearance to the disciples as a group, with the reference to the 'suffering many things and entering into his glory' in the Emmaus road story. But the Jesus who appears to the disciples in Luke is not a glorious figure, as he is in Matthew, but, on the contrary, a very human one. This would seem to indicate that Luke thinks of the resurrection as a kind of two-stage affair, resurrection/ascension. The Jesus who appears to his disciples is the human Jesus brought back to life, a Jesus who continues his ministry with them by instructing them, and who enters into his glory at his ascension. The disciples/apostles then continue his ministry in the world after they have experienced their own baptism/descent of the Spirit.

For Luke the parousia has receded far into the background. True, he maintains it as a formal element in his expectation (Luke 21.27 || Mark 13.26) but he shows little interest in it. Normally he avoids Mark's eschatological references; his interest is clearly in the ongoing work and witness of the church in the world.

The Lukan resurrection narratives as myth

The generation of Christians for which Luke writes is the same as that for which Matthew writes; Luke, therefore, faces the same need for a Christian foundation myth. As does Matthew, Luke also transforms the story of Jesus into a foundation myth of Christian origins. His method is very different from that of Matthew, but it achieves the same purpose. Faced with the destruction of Jerusalem, Luke interprets Jerusalem as the place of the rejection and death of Jesus, the place, therefore, destroyed by God in righteous retribution. But this does not leave the believer bereft in the world. The function of the old sacred centre is now fulfilled by the Christian movement itself in its inevitable progress from Jerusalem to the ends of the earth. The believer within that movement now lives out of his or her relationship to the sacred time of Jesus, and he or she lives, as Jesus lived, by means of the inspiration and power of the Spirit of God. I pointed all this out earlier; I am now simply restating it to claim that this is the Lukan version of the foundation myth of Christian origins.

As in the case of Matthew, I am not claiming that Luke sat down and consciously thought out a Christian foundation myth. What has happened in both instances, in my view, is that the Gospel of Mark was received and used in the community each evangelist represented, and a generation of use of the gospel in circumstances where there was need for a Christian foundation myth – a need Mark had not faced – transformed the story of Jesus into that foundation myth. But the story of Jesus as Mark presents it does not function well as foundation myth. It does not provide a basis upon which subsequent generations can build; rather it confronts each generation with the challenge of its primordial theme and of the parousia. So in the course of time, and ultimately at the hands of the evangelists Matthew and Luke, it is redacted, edited, and transformed, until it does serve that purpose. The major aspect of that redaction, although not the only aspect, is the addition of the resurrection narratives.

In the case of Luke, the resurrection/ascension narratives both set off the time of Jesus as the sacred time and interpret the future course of events for the believer in the world. They make possible, and logical, the addition of the Acts of the Apostles, for Acts tells the story of fulfilment of the words of the risen Lord to his disciples/apostles. When the Christian movement reaches Rome, the symbolic centre for the world, in the form of Paul preaching the gospel 'openly and unhindered' (Acts 28.31), the story is complete and the believers can now identify themselves in the world, and understand the potentialities and responsibilities of their lives in that world.

Now we can see why Luke so resolutely locates all the resurrection appearances in or near Jerusalem. For Matthew the foundation myth comes to a climax in the commissioning of the disciples to form the Christian church, and he believes that this took place in Galilee in fulfilment of the promise of Jesus to his disciples that they would see him in Galilee. But for Luke the essence of the myth is the fate-laden progress of Jesus to Jerusalem, and of the gospel from Jerusalem to Rome. So the resurrection appearances take place in Jerusalem, where the disciples/apostles must stay until they begin the progression from Jerusalem to Rome. The needs of the myth demand it.

The interpretation of the Lukan resurrection narratives

Luke–Acts presents a challenge to the reader quite different from that of the Gospel of Matthew. The Matthaean resurrection narratives challenge the reader to think of religion in terms of response to verbal revelation as authoritatively interpreted by the church, and of life in the world as essentially life in the church, a life sustained by the presence of the risen Lord in the church. The Lukan resurrection narratives, on the other hand, challenge the reader to think of religion in terms of the imitation of Jesus, in terms of accepting responsibility for the gospel as Jesus accepted responsibility for his mission, and in terms of living out of the power of the same Spirit which empowered Jesus. Moreover these narratives, especially the Emmaus road narrative, promise the reader that he or she can know Jesus as risen in the eucharist. To speak of the resurrection in Lukan terms is to speak of the possibility of a life lived in imitation of the example of Jesus, to speak of the possibility of being moved and empowered by the Spirit of God which is the Spirit of Jesus. It is little wonder that Christians of a liberal theological persuasion have always turned instinctively to the Gospel of Luke. For those who think of Jesus as the first Christian – for these people the Gospel of Luke is *the* gospel. The possibility of a life in the world on these terms is the validation of the claim 'Jesus is risen!' To plagiarize Bultmann again, to speak of the resurrection in Lukan terms is to say that Jesus is risen into the life of the believer, and into the common life of the believers.

CONCLUSION

One thing I have not discussed in these pages is the question, 'What actually happened on that first Easter morning?' I have not discussed that question because it is essentially a modern question, alien to these ancient religious texts. None of the gospel writers is concerned to give us what we would call historical information; they are evangelists, not historians. If we demand modern historical information from the gospels, then they become recalcitrant, as we might expect, and as the literature on the subject amply testifies. What actually happened on that first Easter morning, according to the evangelists, is that it became possible to know Jesus as ultimacy in the historicality of the every-day (Mark), that it became possible to live the life of a Christian within the church (Matthew), that it became possible to imitate Jesus in a meaningful life in the world (Luke). With these claims these ancient religious texts became modern, and it is the validity of these claims that must concern us if we are to read the resurrection narratives as the evangelists who wrote them intended them to be read.

But simply to say this is clearly not enough in the modern world. A modern reader most naturally asks the question, 'What actually happened?', and a modern writer on the resurrection or the resurrection narratives must face the challenge of that question. I, as a New Testament scholar, can only claim to be allowed to answer it in terms of the findings of contemporary New Testament scholarship.

In this connection a first thing to do is to locate the New Testament evidence on some kind of a chronological scale. Earliest of all is Paul's testimony in I Cor. 15.3–7.

> For I delivered unto you as of first importance what I also received,

that Christ died for our sins
in accordance with the scriptures,
that he was buried,
that he was raised on the third day
in accordance with the scriptures,
and that he appeared to Cephas,
then to the twelve.
Then he appeared to more than five hundred brethren at one time, most of whom are still alive, though some have fallen asleep.
Then he appeared to James,
then to all the apostles.
Last of all, as to one untimely born,
he appeared also to me.

There is uniform agreement among the scholars that Paul wrote this letter to the Corinthians about AD 55, that is, some twenty or twenty-five years after the death/resurrection of Jesus, but that he was for the most part quoting a liturgical formula which is very much older than the date of his letter. We have no idea as to how old the liturgical formula might be, but it is certainly at least twenty years older than the Gospel of Mark, written about AD 70, and thirty-five to forty years older than the narratives in Matthew or Luke–Acts, written about AD 85–90.

What makes this liturgical statement particularly important to us is not only that it is the earliest statement concerning the resurrection which we possss, although it is that by some twenty years, but also that, in the first place, it lists *appearances* of the risen Jesus to various individuals and groups, and that in the second place, Paul includes himself among those to whom the risen Lord has appeared. Then, thirdly, there is here – and for that matter elsewhere in Paul's letters – no mention of the empty tomb.

All of this has given scholars to think most furiously and the upshot of their thinking may be expressed as follows. First of all, the empty tomb tradition is comparatively late. There is no evidence for any such tradition earlier than the Gospel of Mark, itself written some forty years after the event. Scholars are coming increasingly to the conclusion that the empty tomb tradition is an interpretation of the event – a way of saying 'Jesus is risen!' – rather than a description of an aspect of the event itself. But the matter is very different with regard to the appearances. The more we study the tradition with regard to the appearances the firmer the rock begins to appear upon which they are based.

The most important thing is that we have the actual testimony of Paul himself. He lists himself as one to whom the risen Christ has 'appeared', and there are places in his letters where he talks about this experience, albeit somewhat reluctantly. Incidentally, this reluctance should not be misunderstood. The evidence of his letters indicates that Paul was constantly faced by rival missionaries who boasted of 'experiences', and of 'revelations'. In such a context Paul can be expected to have been guarded in the discussion of his own 'experience'. But there are nonetheless four places where he does allow himself to speak of it, and these places are enormously important to us as places where we actually can hear someone talking about having seen the risen Lord.

The first of these places is the one I have already quoted, I Cor. 15.3–7, where Paul includes himself among the list of those to whom the risen Lord had appeared. The importance of this, for our immediate purpose, is that it shows that Paul equates the appearance to himself with the appearances to Cephas (Peter), the twelve, and others. He thought of himself as having experienced an appearance of the risen Lord, just as they had. In this connection it is perhaps important to remind ourselves quite deliberately to ignore Luke's three accounts of the appearance to Paul on the Damascus road in Acts 9, 21, and 26. These are somebody else's accounts of what happened to Paul, not Paul's own, and like all the narratives in the gospels and in the Acts of the Apostles they are didactic, designed to make theological points, rather than historical, designed to recount 'what actually happened'. But in the case of Paul's letters, we have his own words on the subject.

In addition to the listing of his experience of the risen Lord in I Cor. 15.8 is Paul's reference to this event in Gal. 1.15–16:

> But when he who set me apart before I was born, and had called me through his grace, was pleased to reveal his Son to me, in order that I might preach him among the Gentiles . . .

This is in the context of a passionate defence by Paul of his right to be considered an apostle, and of his right to pursue and to preach the gospel as he understands it, a gospel which 'came through a revelation of Jesus Christ' (Gal. 1.12).

A third reference in Paul's letters is found in a similar context of defence of his apostleship, and for this we return to I Corinthians, to I Cor. 9.1–2.

> Am I not free? Am I not an apostle? Have I not seen Jesus our Lord?

The fourth and last reference is more reflective in nature, being found in one of the best known and most loved passages in Paul's letters, Phil. 3.7–11:

> But whatever gain I had, I counted as loss for the sake of Christ. Indeed I count everything as loss because of the surpassing worth of knowing Christ Jesus my Lord. For his sake I have suffered the loss of all things, and count them as refuse, in order that I may gain Christ and be found in him, not having a righteousness of my own, based on law, but that which is through faith in Christ, the righteousness from God that depends on faith, that I may know him and the power of his resurrection, becoming like him in his death, that if possible I may attain the resurrection from the dead.

These excerpts from the letters of Paul are the most important passages in the New Testament from the standpoint of knowing 'what actually happened' in the case of the resurrection of Jesus, because they are the only instances of someone to whom the risen Jesus actually appeared talking about the event. It is clear from the evidence that the appearance stories are the heart of the matter so far as the evidence for the resurrection of Jesus is concerned. We find such references already in I Corinthians, and in connection with Paul himself, and we have seen that Mark deliberately suppresses any such stories, for theological reasons of his own, so that the fact that the next such stories are found some thirty years later than I Corinthians, in the gospels of Matthew and Luke, no longer surprises us. Also we need not be surprised by the fact that the appearance stories in Matthew and Luke are difficult to reconcile with the list in I Corinthians 15, because we have to reckon not only with the telling and retelling of the stories over a period of some thirty years, but also with the intensive theological motivation of the evangelists Matthew and Luke, which, as we have seen, can most seriously affect their narratives.

So the Christian who asks the modern question, 'What actually happened on that first Easter morning?' must come to terms with the apostle Paul. Paul is the one witness we have whom we can interrogate about his claim to have seen Jesus as risen, and our assumption has to be that if we could interrogate the other witnesses their claims would be similar to his. In some way they were granted a vision of Jesus which convinced them that God had vindicated Jesus out of his death, and that therefore the death of Jesus was by no means the end of the impact of Jesus upon their lives and upon the world in which they lived. Very much to the contrary, since Jesus as risen commissioned them to new tasks and to new responsibilities, they found confidence in themselves and in the future of the world in which they lived precisely because they were responding to Jesus as risen, and because they were now living in a world in which Jesus was risen. If I personally were asked in connection with the resurrection of Jesus, 'What actually happened?', it is in these terms that I would reply.

I am reluctant to say more than that because I believe that I have reached the limits of what the testimony of Paul entitles me to say, and because I am moving far beyond the intent of the gospel narratives. My concern throughout has been the intent of the gospel narratives of the resurrection and here I am glad to close my discussion by affirming once more the intent of those narratives as I understand them. Mark is attempting to convince his readers that they can experience the ultimacy of God in the concreteness, the historicality of their every-day existence; that wherever they are, God is also there, and he is there in the form of the figure of Jesus known from the gospel stories. Matthew is attempting to convince his readers that the eternal ship of the church is the vehicle of salvation for all people everywhere and that aboard that ship the risen Lord effectively sustains those who believe in him. Luke is attempting to convince his readers that Jesus effectively lived out the life of the first Christian in the world and that the resurrection means that his spirit now empowers those who follow him truly to imitate his life. These are the meanings of the resurrection so far as the evangelists are concerned, and as such they are more important than the question of 'What actually happened?' in terms of appearance stories and empty tomb traditions.

POSTSCRIPT

Norman Perrin died in November 1976, while this book was going through the press. 'As in Adam all die, so also in Christ shall all be made alive.'

www.ingramcontent.com/pod-product-compliance
Ingram Content Group UK Ltd.
Pitfield, Milton Keynes, MK11 3LW, UK
UKHW020615180726
13836UKWH00010B/2485